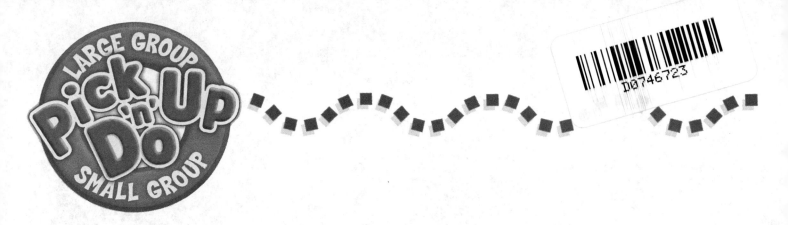

Survivor Bible Style!

12 Instant Bible Lessons for Kids

Edited by Lois Keffer
and Mary Grace Becker

NE✗GEN®

Building the New Generation of Believers

An Imprint of Cook Communications Ministries
COLORADO SPRINGS, COLORADO • PARIS, ONTARIO
KINGSWAY COMMUNICATIONS, LTD., EASTBOURNE, ENGLAND

Pick Up 'n' Do: Survivor Bible Style!
Copyright © 2005 Cook Communications Ministries

All rights reserved. No part of this book may be reproduced in any manner whatsoever without prior written permission from the publisher, except where noted on handouts and the case of brief quotations embodied in critical articles and reviews. For information write to Permissions Editor, Cook Communications Ministries, 4050 Lee Vance View, Colorado Springs, Colorado 80918.

Scripture quotations, unless otherwise noted, are from

THE HOLY BIBLE, NEW INTERNATIONAL VERSION (NIV)
Copyright © 1973, 1978, 1984 by International Bible Society.
Used by permission of Zondervan Publishing House. All rights reserved.

Edited by: Mary Grace Becker, Lois Keffer
Written by: Debbie Allmon, Mary Grace Becker, Kathleen Dowdy, Kim Gunderson, Susan Epperson, Dana Hood, Lindy Keffer, Lois Keffer, Susan Martins Miller, Faye Spieker, Susan Vannaman, Jennifer Wilger, Paula Yingst
Art Direction: Nancy L. Haskins
Cover Design: Helen Harrison
Interior Design: Helen Harrison, Nancy L. Haskins, Lois Keffer
Illustrators: Kris and Sharon Cartwright and Lois Keffer

Printed in the United States

First printing, 2005
1 2 3 4 5 6 7 8 9 10   09 08 07 06 05

ISBN 0781440688

Table of Contents

Quick Start Guide 4

Lesson 1 **Spies-es and Surprises!** 7
Joshua 2:1–6, 8, 12, 13, 17, 18, 21; 6:22

Lesson 2 **The Little Army that Could** 17
Judges 6–7

Lesson 3 **Showdown on Mt. Carmel** 27
1 Kings 18:21–26, 29, 30, 33–36, 38, 39

Lesson 4 **Prophet on the Run** 37
1 Kings 19:2–15, 19

Lesson 5 **Who's Calling?** 47
Isaiah 6:1–8; 9:1–6

Lesson 6 **Hezekiah in a Hot Spot** 57
2 Kings 18:1, 3, 5; 19:10, 11, 14–16, 19, 32–35

Lesson 7 **Treasure in the Temple** 67
2 Kings 22:1–15, 19; 23:1–3, 25

Lesson 8 **The Queen and Mr. Mean** 77
The Book of Esther

Lesson 9 **Way Cool** 87
Daniel 3:1, 4–6, 19, 20, 24–28

Lesson 10 **The Not-So-Hungry Lions** 97
Daniel 6:3–5, 7, 9–11, 13, 14, 16, 17, 19–21, 25, 26

Lesson 11 **Ambush!** 107
Acts 21:30, 33; 22:30; 23:1, 2, 10, 12, 13, 16, 19–24

Lesson 12 **Storm Warning** 117
Acts 27:1, 14, 18–26, 33–36, 42–44

Quick Start Guide

Pick Up 'n' Do elementary lessons give your kids great Bible teaching and serious discipleship without hours of preparation. You and your kids will love these large group/small group lessons. Two options let you take the lesson from super simple to more challenging.

If you're looking for an "instant" lesson that you can pick up and do at the last minute, you've got it in Bible 4U! and Shepherd's Spot.

All you need is a photocopier and basic classroom supplies such as pencils, scissors and glue sticks. Copy the **Bible 4U!** instant drama and the **Shepherd's Spot** handout and you're ready to go.

Are you looking for something beyond the basics?

The optional **Get Set** section of the lessons gives you an opportunity to get a puppet into the action. "Schooner" is a mouthy macaw whose bright remarks will bring giggles and grins each week. And he does a smack-up job of setting up the Bible story.

Don't have a puppet ministry team in your church? How about recruiting middle schoolers? The lively back and forth between Schooner and the Leader is right up their alley. What a great way to get them involved in ministry to younger children!

Bible 4U!

The Bible is full of drama! What better way to teach than with fascinating dramas that take a unique approach to each Bible story? Photocopy the instant drama, pull volunteers from your group to read the roles and you're ready to go.

You'll keep your knowledgeable students engaged, and give kids who are new to God's Word a solid foundation of biblical truth. The dramas call for just a few characters. You may want to play the main role yourself. Or, call on a teen or adult drama troupe to prepare and present the dramas each week. Either way, kids will see the Bible stories come to life in unforgettable ways.

Shepherd's Spot

This is the second essential step of the lesson. After **Bible 4U!**, kids break into small groups with one adult helper for every eight to ten kids. Nothing leaves a more indelible impact on kids' lives than the warm, personal touch of a caring adult. The photocopiable instructions and handouts will give your helpers the confidence they need to help kids consider how to live out what they've learned.

In the **Shepherd's Spot**, kids will read the story straight from the Bible. They'll learn basic Bible skills, and complete a fun, photocopiable handout that helps them understand how to get the story off the page and into their lives. They'll close each week by sharing concerns and praying together.

Workshop Wonders

And there's more! Each week, the optional **Workshop Wonders** section gives you a game, craft, science or cooking activity that gets your kids out of their chairs and into the action.

The **Workshop Wonders** activities require more than the usual classroom supplies. If you choose one of these activities, you'll need to pick up cooking or science ingredients or a few simple craft or game supplies. If you don't mind a little extra preparation, you'll find that there's nothing like a little hands-on action to bring that moment of learning wonder to kids' faces.

These special activities are guaranteed to make a memory and help the Bible lesson stick with kids for a long time to come.

That's it! You can go for a quick, simple lesson with **Bible 4U!** and the **Shepherd's Spot**.

If you wish, add another level of excitement and learning with the Schooner script in the optional **Get Set** section of each lesson.

And if you love teaching with activities, do a little shopping and give kids the memorable experiences of **Workshop Wonders**.

Do you want to give your kids even more great stuff?

How About Staff?

Finding Schooner

If you do the **Get Set** option to open the lessons, you'll need to purchase a parrot or scarlet macaw puppet.

You'll find a great selection on the Internet, in all sizes and prices. Type "scarlet macaw puppet" into your favorite search engine and browse until you find the puppet that suits your price range.

You need just a few helpers to make Pick Up 'n' Do lessons a great experience for you and your kids!

1. A leader/emcee hosts the **Bible 4U!** instant drama each week. For a quick presentation, pull kids from your group to read the roles in the dramas. When there are just one or two parts, you may want to step into the leading role yourself.

2. You may wish to ask a small drama troupe to prepare the stories each week. Five or six volunteers who serve on a rotating basis can easily cover the stories with just a few minutes' preparation.

3. For the **Shepherd's Spot**, you'll need one adult leader for every eight to ten kids. You'll need caring adults in this role—people who are good listeners and feel comfortable sharing their lives with kids. This is a great first step into children's ministry for adults who haven't taught before.

4. If you choose to do the optional **Get Set** puppet script, you'll need a leader and a puppeteer. It's best to use the same leader who hosts the Bible dramas. If you recruit a couple of people to play Schooner, they can rotate every few weeks.

For Overachievers

Do you have a great stage set-up at your church? Then you may want to go for some flash and glitz. Give Schooner a little tropical cabana with a palm tree and a sea-breezy backdrop. Make sure your leader has an obnoxious tropical shirt to slip on.

Don't forget the music! Warm kids up each week with lively, interactive praise songs. Then bring on Schooner's set to the tune of island rhythms.

Equip your drama troupe with a box full of Bibletime costumes. You'll find tips for props and staging in the "for Overachievers" box just before each Bible story. Of course, all this pizzazz is purely optional. The most important ingredient in a wonderful Bible lesson is YOU—the warm, caring leader whose love for kids calls you into children's ministry in the first place! There is absolutely no substitute for the personal attention you give to children each week. You become the model of Jesus himself through your gifts of time and commitment.

God bless you as you minister to his kids!

Spies-es and Surprises!

Get Set

LARGE GROUP ■ Greet kids and do a puppet skit. When Schooner feels like a not-too-nice parrot, he discovers that God can change hearts and give a fresh start.

❑ *large bird puppet* ❑ *puppeteer*

Bible 4U! Instant Drama

LARGE GROUP ■ A woman with a bad reputation saves the lives of two spies who save her life in return.

❑ *4 actors* ❑ *copies of pp. 10-11, Double Rescue script*
❑ *4 numbered balls* Optional: ❑ *red colored rope or crepe paper* ❑ *Bibletime costumes* ❑ *house set (low table, cushions, plants)* ❑ *rocks and trees*

Shepherd's Spot

SMALL GROUP ■ Use the "Welcome Card" handout to help kids create a warm, inviting environment for visitors.

❑ *Bibles* ❑ *pencils* ❑ *scissors* ❑ *copies of p. 14, Welcome Card* ❑ *copies of p. 16, Special Delivery*

Workshop Wonders

SMALL GROUP ■ Make "scarlet cord" breadstick snacks to highlight the faith of a resourceful Rahab.

❑ *refrigerated crescent rolls* ❑ *Parmesan cheese* ❑ *pastry brush* ❑ *melted butter* ❑ *plastic knife* ❑ *egg white* ❑ *paprika* ❑ *sesame seeds* ❑ *cookie sheet* ❑ *oven* Optional: ❑ *taco seasoning*

Bible Basis
Rahab helps the Jewish spies.
Joshua 2:1–6, 8, 12, 13, 17, 18, 21; 6:22

Learn It!
Anyone can come to God.

Live It!
Welcome people to God's family.

Bible Verse
For the Son of Man came to seek and to save what was lost.
Luke 19:10

Quick Tales

2:1 Then Joshua son of Nun secretly sent two spies from Shittim. "Go, look over the land," he said, "especially Jericho." So they went and entered the house of a prostitute named Rahab and stayed there.
2 The king of Jericho was told, "Look! Some of the Israelites have come here tonight to spy out the land."
3 So the king of Jericho sent this message to Rahab: "Bring out the men who came to you and entered your house, because they have come to spy out the whole land."
4 But the woman had taken the two men and hidden them. She said, "The men came to me, but I did not know where they had come from.
5 At dusk, when it was time to close the city gate, the men left. "I don't know which way they went. Go after them quickly. You may catch up with them."
6 (But she had taken them up to the roof and hidden them under the stalks of flax she had laid out on the roof.)

8 Before the spies lay down for the night, she went up on the roof
12 "Now then, please swear to me by the LORD that you will show kindness to my family, because I have shown kindness to you. Give me a sure sign
13 that you will spare the lives of my father and mother, my brothers and sisters, and all who belong to them, and that you will save us from death."
17 The men said to her, "This oath you made us swear will not be binding on us
18 unless, when we enter the land, you have tied this scarlet cord in the window..."
21 "Agreed," she replied. "Let it be as you say." So she sent them away and they departed. And she tied the scarlet cord in the window.
6:22 Joshua said to the two men who had spied out the land, "Go into the prostitute's house and bring her out and all who belong to her, in accordance with your oath to her."

Insights

Throughout scripture, God uses the unlikeliest people to bring about his plans. Rahab certainly fits into this category! The Israelite spies may have chosen to go to Rahab's house for wise reasons. It would not look suspicious to have strange men entering the house of a prostitute; the house was situated on the city wall where the men could see who was coming and going; and the window on the wall might (and did!) offer them a means of escape.

Rahab evidently had great respect for the God of the Israelites. She recounted to the spies her knowledge of events in Egypt forty years earlier and of the Israelites' recent conquest of nearby kingdoms. Even though she lived in a tremendously fortified city, she chose to cast her fate with God's people. And at great risk to herself she gave "aid and comfort" to the advancing enemy. As the attack approached, Rahab convinced her family to take refuge in her house. She gambled all that was dear to her on the word of the Israelite spies and the Lord they served.

After Jericho fell, Rahab and her family would have been required to live outside the Israelite camp. But she eventually adopted the Jewish faith and customs and married an Israelite named Salmon, the great-great grandfather of King David. Rahab's act of faith brought her into the lineage of Jesus himself!

It's sometimes difficult for us to accept the fact that people who are vastly different in habit and appearance can be redeemed and used of God. Use this lesson to teach kids to welcome all who truly seek God.

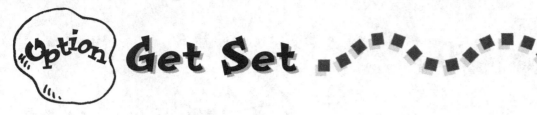

Get Set

Open with lively music, then greet the kids. **I'm a little worried this morning. I haven't seen much of Schooner. He's usually flying around, all excited because you kids are coming. I need to find out what's going on with him. Schooner, are you coming out?** *Schooner pops up.*

Schooner: *(head down, sighs)*
Leader: What's the matter? Where's my cheerful, chipper parrot?
Schooner: I did something mean to the little chickadee down the street.
Leader: Hmm.
Schooner: And now my heart's all achy breaky.
Leader: No matter how you feel, Schooner, all is not lost.
Schooner: No?
Leader: God works through people—even people who make mistakes. We're going to hear about a woman like that in our Bible story today.
Schooner: She messed up, and God still used her?
Leader: Yes. Her name was Rahab and she risked her life to help God's people.
Schooner: She must have been a people-person.
Leader: She had done some pretty bad things in her life as well.
Schooner: And God still loved her?
Leader: God loves everyone.
Schooner: *(hangs head)* I suppose.
Leader: If you want to get back on track, saying "I'm sorry" is always a good place to start.
Schooner: But saying, "I'm sorry" is hard.
Leader: Maybe the little chickadee will help. She might welcome you as a friend.
Schooner: You think?
Leader: When we reach out to people—or chickadees—it's not uncommon for them to reach right back.

Schooner: Well, I know God forgives people who say they're sorry. But I don't know about the chickadee. She'll probably look down her little beak at me for the rest of her life. Besides, I've never been friends with a chickadee before. Chickadees and parrots don't have much in common.
Leader: We don't have to be just like someone else to be friends. After all, the two of us aren't much alike, are we?
Schooner: You're kind of short in the feather department. Your beak is too soft to be good for much. You're not very good at squawking, and you can't fly at all.
Leader: But we're friends. And we both want to learn more about God.
Schooner: I guess you're right.
Leader: Once people turn to God, he can use them to do wonderful things, no matter what their past was like.
Schooner: Sounds like there might be hope for me, then.
Leader: Yep. Just like Rahab in today's Bible story.
Schooner: That's a nice name for a parrot.
Leader: She was a person, not a parrot.
Schooner: Too bad! Let's hear more about it right now in Bible 4U!

Permission to photocopy this script granted for local church use. Copyright © Cook Communications Ministries.
Printed in Pick Up 'n' Do Lessons on Survivor Bible Style!

1 Bible 4U!

Hey, it's good to see everyone. Welcome to Bible 4U!. I hope you're ready to hang on to your seats, because today's story is full of spies and danger and one woman who survived it all. Let's set the stage.

Long before this story took place, God led his people out of slavery in Egypt. Because they grumbled and disobeyed, God didn't let them go right into the land he had promised them. But after forty years the waiting was over. Joshua led the people across the Jordan River and into the Promised Land. The people who lived in the Promised Land worshiped idols, so God gave Joshua orders to drive them out.

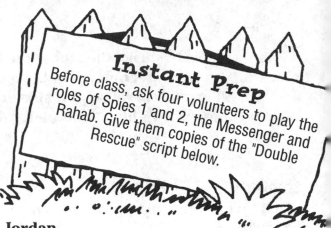

Instant Prep

Before class, ask four volunteers to play the roles of Spies 1 and 2, the Messenger and Rahab. Give them copies of the "Double Rescue" script below.

for Overachievers

Have a four-person drama team prepare the story. Dress Rahab in rich robes; the others can wear typical Bibletime costumes. Prepare a set of Rahab's home with a low table and floor cushions. Create a prominent window.

The city of Jericho was the first big challenge for Joshua's army. It had huge walls nearly twelve feet thick. Joshua decided to send spies into the city to gather intelligence.

It was a risky assignment, and the spies would have been caught if help hadn't come from a surprising source...

Double Rescue
Based on Joshua 2:1–6, 8, 12, 13, 17, 18, 21; 6:22

Spies 1 and 2 sneak on stage, cautiously looking around them.

Spy 1: *(points)* There! We'd probably be safe at that house.

Spy 2: But...but that house belongs to woman who's not a good person.

Spy 1: Men are always coming and going from her house. No one will notice if we slip in.

Spy 2: Okay, if you say so.

They knock on Rahab's door.

Rahab: Gentlemen! Come in, come in. *(Looks them over.)* You're not from around here, are you?

Spy 2: *(nervously)* What makes you say that?

Rahab: Your clothes, the way you talk and the fact that you look nervous enough to jump out of your skin.

Spy 1: *(more calmly)* We're just looking for a place to rest for a few minutes.

Rahab: The Israelites are camped not too far from here. Everyone knows they're planning to attack sometime soon. You wouldn't just happen to be Israelite spies, would you? *There's a loud knock on the door. The spies look at each other and gasp.*

Rahab: That would be a messenger from the king. Someone else must have recognized you as Israelites. Quick—follow me to the roof. I'll hide you.

They follow her and pretend to climb.

Rahab: Lie down and I'll cover you with this flax. *(they lie down and she covers them with sheet)* Don't move and don't make a sound. I'll get rid of the king's messenger.

There's more loud pounding at the door as Rahab pretends to go downstairs.

Messenger: Open up in the name of the king. Open up, I say!

Rahab: *(opens the door)* My, but you're in a hurry.

Messenger: I have an urgent message from the king. Two men came to your house earlier. They're spies! Bring them out.

Rahab: Those men were spies? Oh, my. I didn't think to ask where they came from. They left through the city gate just before dark. I don't know which way they went, but if you go quickly I'm sure you'll be able to find them.

Messenger: Thank you, ma'am. I'll report back to the king. I'm sure he'll reward you for your help.

Messenger goes off. Rahab turns to the spies.

Rahab: Pssst! You can come out now—it's safe.

Spies toss off the sheets.

Spy 1: You saved our lives just now. Why would you risk your life to help us?

Rahab: I know of your God. I've heard all the stories of the great miracles he did to bring your people out of Egypt many years ago. There is no god like the God of Israel. He is God in heaven above and on earth below.

Spy 2: I'm surprised to find someone who believes in the true God in this pagan city.

Rahab: As I have shown kindness to you, please show kindness to me and my family. When your army comes to destroy our city, please spare my family and me.

Spy 1: You saved our lives, we'll save yours.

Rahab: Here—this window looks right over the city wall. I can lower you with this rope. Go into the hills and hide for three days. By then the search party will give up.

Spy 1: If you want us to keep our promise to save you, make sure this scarlet rope is hanging from your window. And have your whole family here in this house.

Rahab: Agreed! Now go, and may your God go with you.

Spies run around the stage and hide behind obstacles or trees.

Spy 1: Pretty slick escape, huh?

Spy 2: Who ever would have thought we'd get help from a woman like Rahab?

Spy 1: That was a surprise. But she really believes in God. I hope we can get her out safely when we attack the city.

Spy 2: Look! There's a search party. Hit the deck!

Spies duck out of sight.

Rahab: *(to the audience)* My story has an ending that will surprise you. When the Israelites marched around Jericho they shouted and the great walls of my city fell down. True to their word, the Israelites saved my whole family and me. Even though I was the woman with the worst reputation in the town of Jericho, God drew me to him and changed me. And through my family the Savior of the world was born. When a lost person is searching for God, be there to guide and welcome. God can change anyone!

Rahab exits.

Permission to photocopy this script granted for local church use. Copyright © Cook Communications Ministries.
Printed in Pick Up 'n' Do Lessons on Survivor Bible Style!

Spies on the roof, spies out the window, a daring rescue and a brand new life. Rahab's survivor story has made her famous for thousands of years! Let's find out what kind of "intel" you picked up from this story.

Toss the four numbered balls to different parts of the room. Bring the kids with the balls to the front one by one and ask these questions. Allow kids to get help from the group if they need it. After each correct answer, let kids drop their balls into a bag.

■ **What did Rahab do to help the two spies?**

■ **What kinds of risks did Rahab take by helping the spies? Why did she do it?**

■ **How did Rahab show that she truly believed in God?**

■ **Why do you think God would choose someone like Rahab to be an ancestor of Jesus?**

I wonder if there are any people like Rahab in your lives. She didn't live a good life, but she wanted to change. She knew a little about God and wanted to know even more about him. Meeting the Israelite spies gave her the chance to take a stand with God's people.

You might see people every day who know they're living the wrong way but don't know how to change. Like the Israelite spies, you can help them take steps in the right direction. A few encouraging words, a shared lunch time, an invitation to a special event at church—these small things can be huge in helping people turn toward God.

God welcomes anyone who truly loves him and wants to change. And we need to be ready to help!

Today in your shepherd groups, you'll get to make something cool to welcome people who have never been with us at church before.

Bible Verse
For the Son of Man came to seek and to save what was lost.
Luke 19:10

Dismiss kids to their shepherd groups.

2 Shepherd's Spot

Gather your small group and help kids find Joshua 2 in their Bibles.

Joshua is the sixth book of the Bible, and it's crammed full of the adventures of God's people as they took over the Promised Land. Rahab's story begins early in the book, just as Joshua was planning to attack the first big city that stood in their way.

Have volunteers take turns reading Joshua 2:1–6, 8, 12, 13, 17, 18, 21; 6:22 aloud. To avoid giggles, read 2:1 yourself and pronounce the name of the town "shi-TEEM." If younger children ask what a prostitute is, explain that she's a woman who spends time with lots of different men instead of faithfully loving a husband of her own.

■ **What do you think it was like for Rahab and her family to have to live outside the Israelite camp?**

■ **What is it like to visit a church or a new group of people for the first time?**

Some folks must have been kind to Rahab because she eventually joined the community and married an Israelite man. Let's take some steps of friendship like those friends of Rahab did. Pass out the "Welcome Card" handouts and have kids begin to cut and fold them according to the instructions.

We can make several of these cards and have them on hand to give to visitors. God cares about people who are far from him. Have a volunteer read Luke 19:10: *"For the Son of Man came to seek and to save what was lost."*

■ **What does this verse mean by "lost"?**

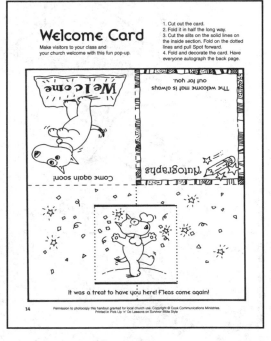

■ **Have you ever been lost? What was that like? How did you get found?**

Rahab got found by God, for he had an important role for her to play. In TV shows, people get voted off their teams. But this is God's story, and Rahab got voted ON to the team!

Invite kids to share prayer concerns. Then close with prayer. **Dear God, we praise you because you don't see us as we are—you see what we can be when we love and obey you. Thank you for the wonderful things that happened in Rahab's life after she believed in you. Help us welcome and guide those who want to know about you, especially** (name people kids shared concerns about). **Help us lead them to you. In Jesus' name, amen.**

Permission to photocopy this lesson page granted for local church use. Copyright © Cook Communications Ministries.
Printed in Pick Up 'n' Do Lessons on Survivor Bible Style!

Welcome Card

Make visitors to your class and
your church welcome with this fun pop-up.

1. Cut out the card.
2. Fold it in half the long way.
3. Cut the slits on the solid lines on the inside section. Fold on the dotted lines and pull Spot forward.
4. Fold and decorate the card. Have everyone autograph the back page.

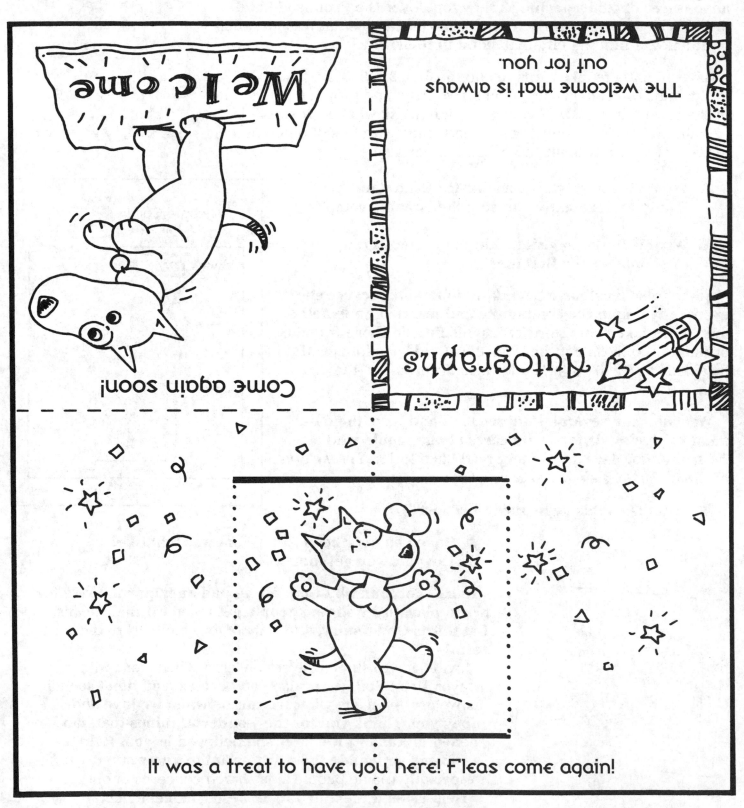

It was a treat to have you here! Fleas come again!

Permission to photocopy this handout granted for local church use. Copyright © Cook Communications Ministries.
Printed in Pick Up 'n' Do Lessons on Survivor Bible Style

Each refrigerated dough can will yield six snacks. Purchase as many as your class needs.

Get List:

- ❑ 8-ounce cans of refrigerated crescent rolls
- ❑ Parmesan cheese (grated)
- ❑ pastry brush
- ❑ melted butter
- ❑ plastic knife
- ❑ egg white
- ❑ paprika
- ❑ sesame seeds
- ❑ cookie sheet
- ❑ oven

Optional
- ❑ Taco seasoning

A scarlet cord hangs from Rahab's window. It's a simple item, but one that saves a faithful Rahab and the lives of her family. Let's make "scarlet cord" snacks as a reminder that brave Rahab took a big risk, changed her life and found a new home with God's people.

On a clean work surface have kids unroll the refrigerated dough. Cut the dough in half and seal the perforations with your fingertips.

Brush one half of the dough with butter. Sprinkle 1/4 cup of Parmesan cheese on top. Place the second dough half on top of the first and press to seal the edges. Cut into six strips. Twist each strip into a cord-like shape.

Place the finished strips on an ungreased cookie sheet. **The color scarlet is brilliant red. In fact, the color scarlet is also know as vermilion, royal red, turkey red, Chinese or Prussian Red, mandarin red—or just plain red!** Brush the strips with egg while. Mix sesame seeds and Parmesan cheese with dashes of paprika or taco seasoning. Sprinkle on the strips. **For our purposes, a dash of the spice paprika will represent the color scarlet.**

Bake the dough strips in a 375º oven for 12 minutes or until golden brown.

■ **What do you think went through Rahab's mind as the Israelite army approached and she hung the scarlet cord from her window?**

■ **What would it be like to lose your home and have to live outside a huge encampment of strangers?**

Rahab saved the lives of the Israelite spies. The cord reminded the approaching army of the promise to keep her safe in the battle to come. That scarlet cord in Rahab's window was like a lifeline. But when the battle was over and Rahab was alone and a stranger outside the Israelite camp, she found a lifeline of people who were willing to teach her about God and welcome her to their families.

As kids enjoy their snacks, challenge them to brainstorm ways they can offer lifelines to people who want to turn to God.

Fold down the corners to start your paper airplane.

SPECIAL DELIVERY

TO

Welcome people to God's family.

Today at church we learned that anyone can come to God. "How did Rahab's story turn into a double rescue? (She saved the spies; the Israelite army saved her.)" How did God reward Rahab? (He gave her a new life and family among the Israelites.)

Bible Verse

For the Son of Man came to seek and to save what was lost.
Luke 19:10

◊ What does it mean to be lost and far from God?

◊ Why do you think God cares so much for the lost, and those who turn their backs on him?

◊ How can you offer a lifeline to people who are searching for God?

Make a treat to welcome a new family on your block, a new friend at school, or visitors to your church. Purchase a bright glass or ceramic mug for each treat. Mix up cupcakes and bake them in the mugs. Use coconut for hair and cinnamon dots to make happy faces on the cupcakes. Tie a little note of welcome with a favorite Bible verse to the hand of the mug. Announce to your new friends that they're about to get "mugged"! Then give them the treats in a mug along with a genuine offer to be friends.

☆ Family FUN

Live It!

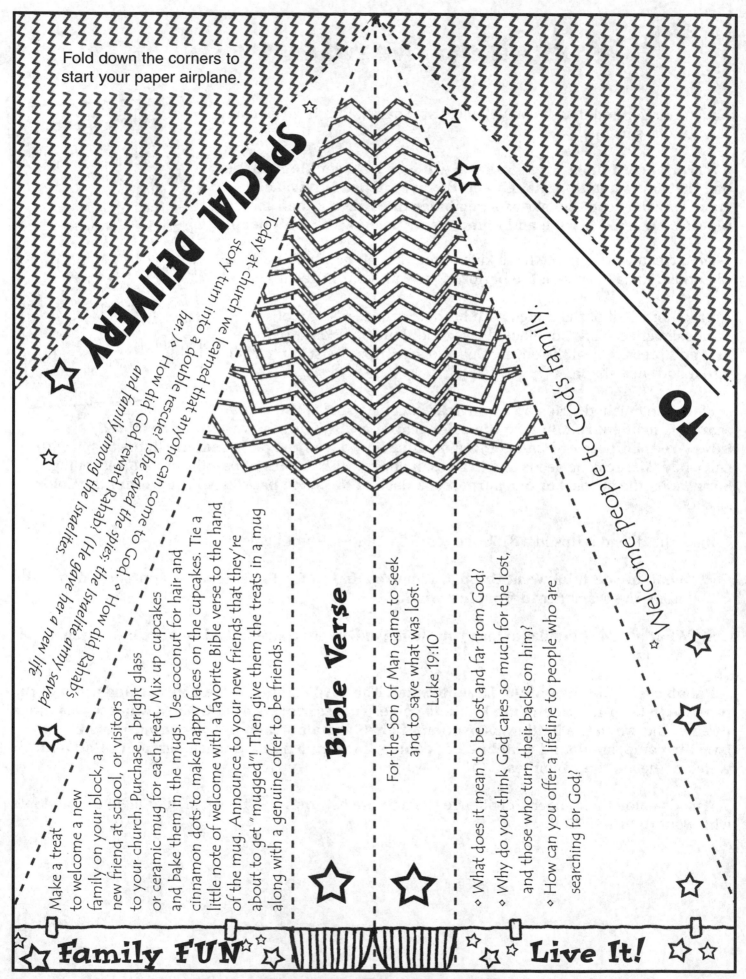

Permission to photocopy this handout granted for local church use. Copyright © Cook Communications Ministries.
Printed in Pick Up 'n' Do Lessons on Survivor Bible Style!

The Little Army that Could

Option

Get Set
LARGE GROUP ■ Greet kids and do a puppet skit. Schooner learns that confidence comes in all sizes.

❏ large bird puppet   ❏ puppeteer

1

Bible 4U! Instant Drama
LARGE GROUP ■ Gideon tells how God used a tiny army to set his people free from powerful enemies.

❏ 5 actors   ❏ copies of pp. 20-21, Ambush! script   ❏ 4 numbered balls
Optional: ❏ rural backdrop   ❏ tent   ❏ Bibletime costumes   ❏ angel costume

2

Shepherd's Spot
SMALL GROUP ■ Use the "Stand Strong" handout to help kids realize that God's power is more than enough for any circumstance.

❏ Bibles   ❏ pencils   ❏ scissors   ❏ copies of p. 24, Stand Strong   ❏ copies of p. 26, Special Delivery

Option

Workshop Wonders
SMALL GROUP ■ Engage in a lopsided balloon battle to demonstrate how we can depend on God's help to defeat a much larger enemy.

❏ air-inflated balloons   ❏ helium balloon tied to a long string   ❏ cardboard box

Bible Basis
Gideon defeats the Midianites.
Judges 6–7

Learn It!
God uses the small to defeat the great.

Live It!
Have confidence in God.

Bible Verse
Finally, be strong in the Lord and in his mighty power.
Ephesians 6:10

Quick Takes

Whenever the Israelites planted their crops, the Midianites, Amalekites and other eastern peoples invaded the country. They camped on the land and ruined the crops all the way to Gaza and did not spare a living thing for Israel, neither sheep nor cattle nor donkeys. Midian so impoverished the Israelites that they cried out to the LORD for help. (6:3-4, 6)

When the angel of the LORD appeared to Gideon, he said, "The LORD is with you, mighty warrior."

"But sir," Gideon replied, "if the LORD is with us, why has all this happened to us?" The LORD turned to him and said, "Go in the strength you have and save Israel out of Midian's hand. Am I not sending you?"

"But Lord," Gideon asked, "how can I save Israel? My clan is the weakest in Manasseh, and I am the least in my family." The LORD answered, "I will be with you, and you will strike down all the Midianites together." (6: 11–13, 15, 16)

Then the Spirit of the LORD came upon Gideon, and he blew a trumpet, summoning the Abiezrites to follow him. (6:34)

But the LORD said to Gideon, "There are still too many men. Take them down to the water, and I will sift them out for you there...So Gideon took the men down to the water. There the LORD told him, "Separate those who lap the water with their tongues like a dog from those who kneel down to drink." The LORD said to Gideon, "With the three hundred men that lapped I will save you and give the Midianites into your hands. Let all the other men go, each to his own place." (7:2–4, 7)

Dividing the three hundred men into three companies, he placed trumpets and empty jars in the hands of all of them, with torches inside. Gideon and the hundred men with him reached the edge of the camp at the beginning of the middle watch, just after they had changed the guard. They blew their trumpets and broke the jars that were in their hands. The three companies blew the trumpets and smashed the jars. Grasping the torches in their left hands and holding in their right hands the trumpets they were to blow, they shouted, "A sword for the LORD and for Gideon!" While each man held his position around the camp, all the Midianites ran, crying out as they fled. (7:16, 19, 20, 21)

Insights

It was the worst of times for Israel. For seven years their old enemies, the Midianites, swept down from the desert at harvest time and plundered their livestock and crops. The Israelites were so helpless against the Midianites' overwhelming numbers that when the raids began, they would head for the hills and hide in caves. These years of oppression left the Israelites impoverished and starving. They needed a hero.

It is so like God to choose the unlikeliest person. Gideon was from the most insignificant family of the smallest tribe of Israel. When an angel called him to the task of driving out the Midianites, Gideon was hiding in a winepress where he couldn't be seen threshing his wheat and so would be safe from passing Midianite marauders.

Gideon was fairly certain God had chosen the wrong man for the job. After God gave him several signs, Gideon consented to form an army. On the eve of battle, God shrank Gideon's already outnumbered army to only 300 men. But clever tactics threw the enemy into confusion and they fled. As the tiny army defeated the massive one, God showed once again that he is God, and no human force can stand against him.

It's easy for kids to be overwhelmed by forces at work around them. This lesson encourages kids to believe that with God's power, the weak can conquer the powerful and God will set things right.

Open with lively music, then greet the kids. **Who me? Couldn't be! That sums up today's Bible story. Yet God uses the small to defeat the great. We are to have confidence in God. Schooner, come and spread a little confidence our way!** *Schooner pops up.*

Schooner: Confidence runs in my family, boss.
Leader: I see.
Schooner: On my mother's side. It's in the genes.
Leader: I didn't know you wore jeans, Schooner.
Schooner: You're teasing me, aren't you?
Leader: A tiny bit. I have a "what if" question for you today, Schooner.
Schooner: Yes?
Leader: What if...all the confident parrots you know went for a swim.
Schooner: Parrots are not swimmers, but we can pretend if you'd like.
Leader: Thank you. So...one day a group of confident parrots go for a swim.
Schooner: The sun is shining and the flowers are blooming. And happy and confident parrots go for a swim! The end.
Leader: Hey, I'm not done. Whose story is this anyway?
Schooner: Sorry, boss. Please continue.
Leader: *(continues)* Suddenly, a crocodile pulls up beside them.
Schooner: A...a...crocodile?
Leader: Let's make that two crocodiles!
Schooner: *(shakes)* Let's not, boss.
Leader: Mr. and Mrs. Crocodile swim closer and closer to the parrots. Here's my question. Just how long would parrot confidence last in such a situation?
Schooner: That's simple. Not long!
Leader: I agree.
Schooner: Being the main entree for a crocodile's lunch is not my idea of a good time.
Leader: Of course not. But I do have a point.
Schooner: The one on top of your head?
Leader: *(rolls eyes)* No, not that one.
Schooner: Let's hear it—quick!

Leader: It's easy to be confident when things are going swimmingly.
Schooner: *(shakes head)*
Leader: In today's Bible story, God asks Gideon, a rather unimportant field hand, to do something that he feels is just too big for him. And it's dangerous work.
Schooner: Count me out, boss.
Leader: But you don't know the rest of the story.
Schooner: Wanna know what I think? Let the little people do the little things and let the big people take care of the rest.
Leader: But that's not always how God works. Sometimes he uses little guys for big things.
Schooner: But we're small!
Leader: And afraid.
Schooner: And don't forget small!
Leader: You already said that.
Schooner: Gulp! This time I mean it!
Leader: In today's story, God uses the small to defeat the great.
Schooner: Really! Like parrots winning over crocodiles.
Leader: Exactly like that. It's all about having confidence in God and his mighty power.
Schooner: I just gotta hear the end of this story, boss.
Leader: Then let's go straight to Bible 4U!

Permission to photocopy this script granted for local church use. Copyright © Cook Communications Ministries.
Printed in Pick Up 'n' Do Lessons on Survivor Bible Style!

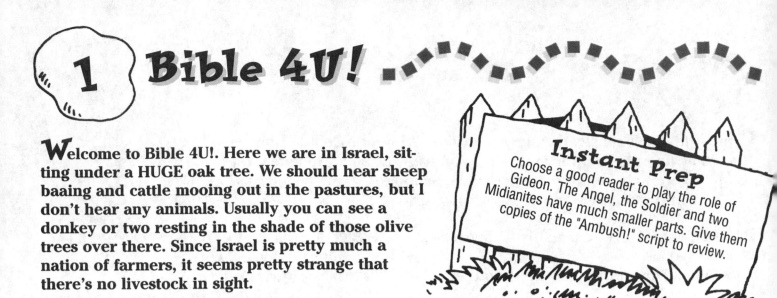

1 Bible 4U!

Welcome to Bible 4U!. Here we are in Israel, sitting under a HUGE oak tree. We should hear sheep baaing and cattle mooing out in the pastures, but I don't hear any animals. Usually you can see a donkey or two resting in the shade of those olive trees over there. Since Israel is pretty much a nation of farmers, it seems pretty strange that there's no livestock in sight.

Instant Prep

Choose a good reader to play the role of Gideon. The Angel, the Soldier and two Midianites have much smaller parts. Give them copies of the "Ambush!" script to review.

See those fields over there? They're stripped bare. They should be filled with stalks of golden wheat and barley waving in the wind. There used to be a grape arbor over that way, with heavy clusters of yummy, purple grapes hanging from the vines. The scent of fruit ripening in the warm sun is so delicious. But the grapevines are bare.

for Overachievers

Have your five-person drama team prepare the story. Create a rural backdrop with a large oak tree as the centerpiece. Place a stool on one side for Gideon. Dress the actors in simple Bibletime costumes. Set up a small tent to one side to represent the Midianite camp.

The whole place looks like somebody came and stole all the livestock and ripped up the crops and left the people to starve.

What are these people going to do?

Ambush!
Based on Judges 6–7

Gideon enters and sits on the stool.

Gideon: *(to audience)* So there I was, hiding in a winepress—a big stone vat—threshing wheat. In normal times I would thresh wheat out in a big open space so all the chaff could blow away. But these aren't normal times. Every year we tend our herds and plant our crops. And every year just before harvest the Midianites come sweeping down out of the hills and steal everything—our grain, our livestock, the grapes off the vines. There's nothing we can do but go up into the hills and hide until the Midianites go away. Our farms and homes are ruined and our people are hungry.

Angel: *(enters and addresses Gideon)* The Lord is with you, mighty warrior.

Gideon: *(looks around)* That was an angel talking. He appeared to me right there in the winepress. I was pretty sure he had the wrong guy. I'm nobody—just an ordinary guy from a small family.

Angel: Go in the strength you have and save Israel from the Midianites. I am sending you. I will be with you and you will strike down the Midianites. *(Exits.)*

Gideon: How could I lead a fight against the Midianites? They have camels and so many fighting men you can't even count them. But the angel showed me that God meant business, so I put out a call for troops.

Soldier: *(enters and speaks to Gideon)* The men from five tribes have answered your call, Gideon. We're ready to follow you into battle. *(Exits.)*

Gideon: I led my men to a campsite by a spring. Then I got a very strange message from God.

Angel: *(enters)* You have too many men. When you win this battle, I want everyone to know that it's by God's power, not your own. Let anyone who is scared go home.

Gideon: So I made the announcement that anyone who was scared of fighting could go home. Twenty-two thousand men left. That left us only 10,000 fighters.

Angel: You still have too many men. Take them down to the water to drink. If anyone kneels to drink, send him home. Keep only the men who lap the water like a dog.

Gideon: Lappers and kneelers. Can you guess how that came out? Nearly all the men went down on their knees to drink. Only 300 men lapped the water. And those 300 were the only ones who got to stay.

Soldier: *(enters; doesn't see Angel)* Um, Gideon? Have you noticed that there are only 300 of us left?

Gideon: He had a point. What could 300 men do against a huge army? Then I realized—we weren't just 300 men. We were 300 men plus God!

Angel: Sneak down to the Midianite camp and listen to what they're saying. You'll be encouraged by what you hear.

Gideon and Soldier sneak over to the Midianite tent and listen.

Midianite 1: Ooh—I just had a terrible dream!

Midianite 2: What did you dream about?

Midianite 1: A monstrous loaf of bread came rolling into camp and smashed our tent to smithereens.

Midianite 2: Oh no! That can only mean one thing. Gideon and his God are going to defeat us. We're toast.

Gideon and Soldier tiptoe back.

Gideon: The Midianites were scared to death! I knew it was time to attack. God gave me an idea for an ambush. Every man got a sword, a trumpet and a torch hidden inside a clay pot.

Soldier: This is pretty strange equipment for going into battle.

Gideon: On my signal we all blew the trumpets. Then we smashed the pots and lifted the burning torches. The men shouted, "For the Lord and for Gideon!" In confusion the Midianites started fighting each other and running away.

Midianite soldiers yell in fear and run in all directions trying to escape.

Soldier: We beat them! With only 300 men we beat them and chased them all the way to the river!

Gideon: Actually, God beat them. We just followed instructions.

Midianites peek from the side.

Midianite 1: *(panting)* Did you see all those Israelite soldiers? They had a huge army. It came out of nowhere!

Midianite 2: I know. I think we were the only ones to get away.

Midianite 1: We won't be attacking them again for a long, long time. *They exit.*

Permission to photocopy this script granted for local church use. Copyright © Cook Communications Ministries.
Printed in Pick Up 'n' Do Lessons on Survivor Bible Style!

Gideon didn't think of himself as a mighty warrior, but that's what the angel called him. Before he knew it, he was leading an itty-bitty army into battle against an overpowering enemy. And guess what—he not only survived, he won! Let's see what you remember about Gideon's ambush.

Toss four numbered balls to different areas of the room. Invite the kids with the balls to come up front one-by-one and answer a question. Allow kids to get help from the group if they need it. After each correct answer, have kids drop their balls into a bag.

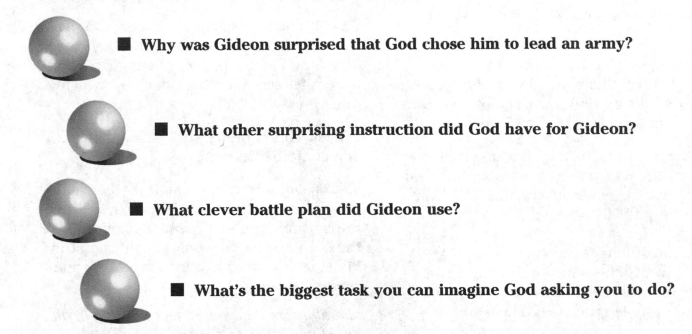

■ Why was Gideon surprised that God chose him to lead an army?

■ What other surprising instruction did God have for Gideon?

■ What clever battle plan did Gideon use?

■ What's the biggest task you can imagine God asking you to do?

But God had a plan in mind, and Gideon was the man for the job. He wanted a leader that would follow his instructions, no matter how strange they might seem. He gave Gideon a teensy-weensy army so that when they won, everyone would know God was behind it. And, boy, did God's plan ever work! When the trumpets blew, the clay pots broke and the flames of the torches blazed in the night, the Midianites got so confused and frightened that they started fighting themselves. And then they ran, and didn't trouble the Israelites for years and years.

The Lord God proved to the Israelites that he could use the small to defeat the great. Today in your shepherd groups, you'll explore what it means to have confidence in God.

Dismiss kids to their shepherd groups.

Bible Verse
Finally, be strong in the Lord and in his mighty power.
Ephesians 6:10

2 Shepherd's Spot

Gather your small group and help kids find Judges 6–7 in their Bibles.

Judges is a book of ups and downs. When the Israelite people followed God, things went well. When they turned away from God and worshiped idols, God allowed their enemies to overrun them. When their hearts turned back to God, he would send a leader like Gideon to make the nation strong again. Let's look at some highlights from Gideon's story.

Have volunteers take turns reading Judges 6:1–6, 11–16, 33–35, 7:2–7, 9–11, 13–21 aloud.

■ **Suppose you were one of the 300 soldiers who remained. What would you have thought when all the others left?**

■ **Why did God want Gideon to go to battle with only 300 men?**

When God looks for leaders, he doesn't necessarily pick the strongest or the smartest. He looks for people who will trust him and have confidence to carry out his commands.

Pass out the "Stand Strong" handout. Have a volunteer read Ephesians 6:10 aloud: *"Finally, be strong in the Lord and in his mighty power."* **That's a pretty good description of what Gideon did, isn't it! Let's put this verse so its words pop right off the page!** Lead kids through the assembly instructions on the handout.

Stand Strong

Like Gideon, you can be strong in God's mighty power!

1. Cut out the box, the words "STRONG" and "MIGHTY POWER" and the springs.
2. To fold the top and bottom, fold forward on the inside lines and back on the outside lines.
3. To fold the sides, fold forward on the outside lines and back on the inside lines.
4. Accordion-fold the springs and glue them to the boxes.
5. Glue "STRONG" to the top spring.
6. Glue "MIGHTY POWER" to the bottom spring.

STRONG MIGHTY POWER

{spring}

{spring}

Finally, be
glue spring here
in the Lord and in his
glue spring here

Ephesians 6:10

24   Permission to photocopy this handout granted for local church use. Copyright © Cook Communications Ministries.
Printed in Pick Up 'n' Do Lessons on Survivor Bible Style!

■ **What's the difference between being strong in your own power and being strong in God's power?**

■ **When do you need to have confidence that God will come through as he has promised?**

Let's pray about times when you need confidence in God. Allow kids to share other prayer requests as well, then close with prayer. **Father, we know that you are the God of Gideon. And like Gideon, it's easy for us to see how big our problems are. Help us to have confidence in you. We pray especially for** (mention kids' concerns). **Help us to be strong in your mighty power this week, amen.**

Permission to photocopy this lesson page granted for local church use. Copyright © Cook Communications Ministries.
Printed in Pick Up 'n' Do Lessons on Survivor Bible Style!

Stand Strong

Like Gideon, you can be strong in God's mighty power!

1. Cut out the box, the words "STRONG" and "MIGHTY POWER" and the springs.
2. To fold the top and bottom, fold forward on the inside lines and back on the outside lines.
3. To fold the sides, fold forward on the outside lines and back on the inside lines.
4. Accordion-fold the springs and glue them to the boxes.
5. Glue "STRONG" to the top spring.
6. Glue "MIGHTY POWER" to the bottom spring.

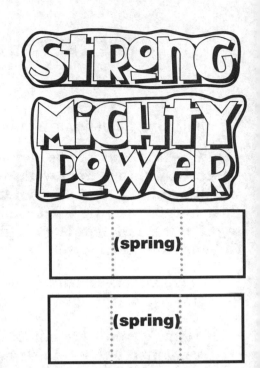

(spring)

(spring)

Finally, be

glue spring here

in the Lord and in his

glue spring here

EPHESIANS 6:10

24   Permission to photocopy this handout granted for local church use. Copyright © Cook Communications Ministries.
Printed in Pick Up 'n' Do Lessons on Survivor Bible Style!

Workshop Wonders

Before class, conceal the helium-filled balloon in a box. Place the box out of sight until later in the activity. **What a crazy battle! Gideon headed off to fight the Midianites with nothing but torches, trumpets and jars. Let's have our own crazy battle to remind us why Gideon was so confident with his tiny army outfitted with unusual weapons.**

Get List:
- ❑ air-inflated balloons (one for every 4-5 children)
- ❑ helium balloon tied to a long string
- ❑ cardboard box

Form teams of four or five children. Give each group an air-inflated balloon.

Okay soldiers, it is time to go to battle. First we need a little training. Your team's mission is to keep the balloon in the air. Combat Rule #1: Each team member can hit the balloon only once. In other words, your group will have to work together to win! If the balloon falls to the ground, your team has lost the battle and you must leave the game. Let's practice.

Let kids play until only one group is left.

You did great! Now it's time for the real balloon-battle! But first I need to make one final adjustment to our teams. Ask for a volunteer to be a one-person team. Speak to that individual. **I'm sorry to say you'll have to keep a balloon in the air all by yourself.**

■ **Do you think** (name) **will be able to keep the balloon in the air as long as the other teams? What are his/her chances of success?**

Have the teams begin play. After a short time, retrieve the box you brought to class. Open it slightly and have your solitary soldier pull out the helium-filled balloon by the string. Wait a while as other teams notice the clear advantage given this small one-member army!

Version 2: For more challenging (yet contained) play, have kids sit in game circles.

■ **Do you think** (name) **has a good chance to win? What's his/her big advantage?**

You've got it! Our soldier here won't have anything to do but hold the string to win the game. A simple weapon, helium gas, makes all the difference.

■ **How is having a helium balloon like having confidence in what God can do?**

Right! It didn't matter how small Gideon's army was or what weapons he used. With God on his side he could go into battle with confidence. This is as true for us as it was for Gideon and his army. Can you remember today's Bible verse? Let's close by saying it aloud together. These are your "marching orders" for the week!

"Finally, be strong in the Lord and in his mighty power" Ephesians 6:10.

Permission to photocopy this lesson page granted for local church use. Copyright © Cook Communications Ministries.
Printed in Pick Up 'n' Do Lessons on Survivor Bible Style!

Fold down the corners to start your paper airplane.

SPECIAL DELIVERY

TO

Have confidence in God.

Today at church we learned from the story of Gideon that the small can defeat the great. "Do you think you would recognize an angel from God? What might a messenger from God look like?"

Our Bible verse tells us to be strong in the Lord and in his mighty power. With God's strength, we can do things we'd never dream of doing on our own. For instance, can a flimsy drinking straw poke through a solid, uncooked potato? Try it. Tough, isn't it? Now put your thumb over the end of the straw and watch it go right into the potato. The secret? The air pressure caused by covering the end of the straw makes it stronger. God is the strength we need. Walk in his power!

Bible Verse

Finally, be strong in the Lord and in his mighty power.
Ephesians 6:10

◊ When does it feel like our family is a small army up against a great big foe?

◊ What are some daily steps we can take to "be strong in the Lord"?

☆ Family FUN

Live It!

26   Permission to photocopy this handout granted for local church use. Copyright © Cook Communications Ministries.
Printed in Pick Up 'n' Do Lessons on Survivor Bible Style!

Showdown on Mt. Carmel

Get Set

Option

LARGE GROUP ■ Greet kids and do a puppet skit. Schooner rethinks his "super parrot" image and listens to the wisdom of God's Word.

❑ *large bird puppet* ❑ *puppeteer*

Bible 4U! Instant Drama

1

LARGE GROUP ■ Two prophets of Baal are taken by surprise at the outcome of Elijah's challenge.

❑ *3 actors* ❑ *copies of pp. 30-31, Baal Fails script* ❑ *4 numbered balls*
Optional: ❑ *Bibletime costumes* ❑ *small table set with food* ❑ *large boxes painted to resemble altars* ❑ *red, yellow and orange crepe paper streamers*

Shepherd's Spot

2

SMALL GROUP ■ Use the "Fire on the Altar" handout to help kids learn why we worship only the one true God.

❑ *Bibles* ❑ *pencils* ❑ *scissors* ❑ *copies of p. 34, Fire on the Altar* ❑ *copies of p. 36, Special Delivery*

Workshop Wonders

Option

SMALL GROUP ■ Simple office supplies make cute little figures for fun— not worship.

❑ *erasers in all shapes, sizes and colors* ❑ *miscellaneous office supplies*

Bible Basis
1 Kings 18:21–26, 29, 30, 33–36, 38, 39

Learn It!
Our God is the only true God.

Live It!
Worship God.

Bible Verse
O LORD God Almighty, who is like you? You are mighty, O LORD, and your faithfulness surrounds you. Psalm 89:8

Quick Takes

18:21 "How long will you waver between two opinions? If the LORD is God, follow him; but if Baal is God, follow him." But the people said nothing.
22 Then Elijah said to them, "I am the only one of the LORD's prophets left, but Baal has four hundred and fifty prophets.
23 Get two bulls for us. Let them choose one for themselves, and let them cut it into pieces and put it on the wood but not set fire to it. I will prepare the other bull and put it on the wood but not set fire to it.
24 Then you call on the name of your god, and I will call on the name of the LORD. The god who answers by fire—he is God." Then all the people said, "What you say is good."
25 Elijah said to the prophets of Baal, "Choose one of the bulls and prepare it first, since there are so many of you. Call on the name of your god, but do not light the fire."
26 So they took the bull given them and prepared it. Then they called on the name of Baal from morning till noon. "O Baal, answer us!" they shouted. But there was no response; no one answered. And they danced around the altar they had made.
29 Midday passed, and they continued their frantic prophesying until the time for the evening sacrifice. But there was no response, no one answered, no one paid attention.
30 Then Elijah said to all the people, "Come here to me." They came to him, and he repaired the altar of the LORD, which was in ruins.
33 He arranged the wood, cut the bull into pieces and laid it on the wood. Then he said to them, "Fill four large jars with water and pour it on the offering and on the wood."
34 "Do it again," he said, and they did it again. "Do it a third time," he ordered, and they did it the third time.
35 The water ran down around the altar and even filled the trench.
36 At the time of sacrifice, the prophet Elijah stepped forward and prayed: "O LORD, God of Abraham, Isaac and Israel, let it be known today that you are God in Israel and that I am your servant and have done all these things at your command.
38 Then the fire of the LORD fell and burned up the sacrifice, the wood, the stones and the soil, and also licked up the water in the trench.
39 When all the people saw this, they fell prostrate and cried, "The LORD —he is God! The LORD he is God!"

Insights

Israel's history centers on a centuries-long tug of war. Would they follow the Lord God or would they be seduced by local gods—idols of wood and stone? Baal worship involved ritual sex and sensuality. It was hard for the Israelites to turn away from such blatant temptation and remain faithful to a God who is high and holy.

Ahab and Jezebel led God's people into one of the most immoral periods in Israel's history. Prophets of Baal were special favorites of the queen and ate at the royal table. Alone and outnumbered, Elijah called the people back to God. When the nation remained unfaithful, God sent a terrible drought on the land. The king blamed Elijah, who challenged the prophets of Baal to a showdown on Mt. Carmel.

Both sides would offer sacrifices. Whoever answered by sending fire to consume the sacrifice was the true God. The prophets of Baal prayed and carried on for hours with no response. But when Elijah prayed, fire fell from heaven. The awed people cried, "The Lord—he is God!"

Kids today still face challenges to God's existence. Use this lesson to assure them that there is no God but our God, and that he is worthy of their worship.

Option Get Set

Open with lively music, then greet the kids. **God our Father rules over heaven and earth. He is big—his power is bigger than a sports stadium! Yet he is small—because he lives in our hearts. Let's worship our one true spectacular God. Schooner, come join the group.** *Schooner pops up.*

Schooner: *(clears throat)* I have something to say.

Leader: And why should today be any different than any other day?

Schooner: This is very important, boss. If I don't say it, I'll just burst.

Leader: By all means, don't do that!

Schooner: Here goes…*(clears throat and announces loudly)* Let it be known here and now that out of all the parrots in the world I am Parrot Supreme!

Leader: Parrot supreme? Schooner, you sound like a pizza topping.

Schooner: Do not!

Leader: A pineapple dessert then.

Schooner: Doooo not!

Leader: Do too.

Schooner: Hey, wait a minute…

Leader: Schooner, where did you hear such a thing?

Schooner: On TV. There were these two big dinosaurs, see? And one said he was king of the universe but the other said he was Ruler Supreme, which everybody knows beats out a silly old king any day…

Leader: Oh, brother!

Schooner: So if a dinosaur can be supreme then a parrot can too. *Squawk!*

Leader: This sounds like an excellent place to introduce today's Bible story.

Schooner: Does it have a Ruler Supreme?

Leader: Our one true God.

Schooner: Oh. He's the biggest!

Leader: In today's Old Testament story not all people believed in our God. They worshiped fake gods made of wood and stone.

Schooner: Fake gods? No way!

Leader: The prophet Elijah tried to tell them, but they wouldn't listen. So he challenged the prophets of the false gods to a showdown.

Schooner: Oh boy! Like cowboys in the street seeing who could draw the fastest?

Leader: Even more exciting than that. It started out with the odds 450 to one.

Schooner: No way!

Leader: Let's make that 450 to one plus God.

Schooner: Oh—that changes everything! So what happened?

Leader: Cool stuff! Fire from heaven for one thing. God left no doubt in the people's minds that he is the only true God.

Schooner: I love it when that happens. So they learned that God is who he says he is.

Leader: Right—he's the one true God.

Schooner: That's a lot better than being the Parrot Supreme. I mean, I'm just an ordinary parrot after all.

Leader: You're a pretty special parrot, I'd say.

Schooner: Thanks, but I think I got a little carried away.

Leader: By a great big dinosaur!

Schooner: The people of Israel got carried away too when they worshiped fake gods instead of the real one.

Leader: Very good point, Schooner.

Schooner: Can we hear the rest of the story, please?

Leader: Bible 4U! up next.

Permission to photocopy this script granted for local church use. Copyright © Cook Communications Ministries.

Printed in Pick Up 'n' Do Lessons on Survivor Bible Style!

1 Bible 4U!

Instant Prep

Before class, ask two older boys to play the roles of Zophar and Azariah. Ask a younger boy or girl to play the role of Elijah. Give all three kids copies of the "Baal Fails" script below.

Welcome back to Bible 4U! In our long march through Bible history, we've now reached the time of prophets and kings. A prophet's job was to deliver God's message. But back in those days, prophets also worked for kings. And the king usually didn't like it when the prophet gave him bad news—even if the prophet was only doing his job by saying what God told him to say. Some kings—and queens, Jezebel in particular—got so mad when they heard bad news that they got rid of the prophets. Permanently.

for Overachievers

Have a three-person drama team prepare the story. Set up a small table with fancy dishes. Create altars from boxes. Have extras slide them into place during the story. Have a helper behind Elijah's altar wave crepe paper streamers to simulate the fire from heaven.

At the time of our story, Queen Jezebel and King Ahab were down to their last true prophet: Elijah. Elijah kept right on giving the news God told him to give, good or bad. Meanwhile, Jezebel had rounded up a whole herd of false prophets. You know how you can tell if a prophet is a false prophet? He only gives good news. All the time. And is life really like that? We know better!

After a while, God told Elijah it was time to settle the score—to prove that the false prophets were powerless against the one, true God. Here come two of Jezebel's false prophets now. Let's see what Elijah is up against.

Baal Fails
Based on 1 Kings 18:21–26, 29, 30, 33–36, 38, 39

Zophar: (looking up) Dude…think it'll rain soon?

Azariah: Dunno…let's ask Baal.

Zophar: Okay…ready?

Both close their eyes tightly and put their fingers on their temples as if concentrating.

Azariah: So, think it'll rain soon?

Zophar: Dunno…does it look like rain?

Both look up.

Together: Nah!

Zophar: Let's get some lunch. I'm sick of standing around here praying for rain.

Azariah: Yeah, sometimes being a prophet of Baal is really boring.

Zophar: You got that right. You know, we could use a little excitement around here. Maybe after lunch a whole bunch of us could do some acrobatics.

Azariah: Yeah. If all 450 of us were standing on our heads, balancing jars of water on our toes, like, do you think Baal would get the message?

Zophar: Cool idea, A. Let's get up to Queen J's for lunch. Wonder what's on the menu?

Azariah: Dunno, but palace food is mighty tasty. We're livin' the good life…if it would just rain.

Zophar: Yeah, yeah, yeah. C'mon.

Both walk across the room and sit down to eat.

Azariah: Hey Z, did you hear that?

Zophar: *(talking with his mouth full)* Hear what?

Azariah: Jehoram just said that Elijah guy is demanding a challenge.

Zophar: Who?

Azariah: You know—Elijah.

Zophar: Oh, him. The prophet who says he serves the one true God. What a loser! His kind are almost gone, thanks to our dear queen. I'll bet Elijah doesn't last too much longer.

Azariah: Well get this: Elijah wants to set up dueling sacrifices.

Zophar: What's a dueling sacrifice?

Azariah: Like, we cut up a bull and he cuts up a bull. We lay out some wood and he lays out some wood.

Zophar: We light ours on fire and he lights his on fire. What's the point?

Azariah: We don't light ours on fire.

Zophar: We don't?

Azariah: Nope. And he doesn't either.

Zophar: That's too weird.

Azariah: We pray to Baal, he prays to Yahweh. Whoever sends the fire wins the duel.

Zophar: That shouldn't be too hard. Dude, we've got 450 prophets, and he's got one. He's toast!

Azariah: Looks like they've got the sacrifice ready. Let's see if we can get Baal's attention.

They wave their hands and dance around. Elijah enters.

Elijah: Hey, you know…nothing much is happening here. Maybe Baal is taking a nap, or deep in thought, or…you know…making a pit stop. I'd try praying a little louder if I were you.

Zophar and Azariah gradually slow their dancing.

Zophar: I'm ready for a break. Let Elijah have his turn. He won't do any better than we did.

Elijah begins to set up his altar.

Azariah: Why is he digging a ditch around that altar?

Zophar: Who knows?

Azariah: Okay—everything's ready. The wood, the bull…

Zophar: Whoa—they're pouring water over the altar. How will it ever catch fire when it's all wet?

Zophar: Four jars full of water. There's no way that thing will light.

Azariah: He's dumber than we thought. We're totally going to stomp him.

Elijah: *(kneeling)* Lord, you are the God of Abraham, Isaac and Israel. Today let everyone know that you are God in Israel. Let them know I'm your servant. Let them know I've done all of these things because you commanded me to. Answer me. Lord, answer me. Then these people will know that you are the one and only God. They'll know you are turning their hearts back to you again.

Toss red, yellow and orange streamers onto the altar. Zophar and Azariah stagger backward and shield their faces.

Zophar: Fire!

Azariah: It's burning up the whole thing!

Zophar: Um…looks like we're the losers.

Azariah: And we'd better get out of here. Do you hear what the people are saying?

Zophar: Yep. "The Lord—he is God! The Lord—he is God."

Azariah: I am so outta here.

Both run away.

Elijah: *(shouting)* Go after them! Don't let them get away! *(to kids)* There is only one true God. People in your day still doubt him. But if you look around, you can see his power all around you—in thunder and lightning, in the motion of the sea, in the songs of birds, in the smile of the person sitting next to you. God created everything—there is no one like him. God rules!

Elijah exits.

Permission to photocopy this script granted for local church use. Copyright © Cook Communications Ministries. Printed in Pick Up 'n' Do Lessons on Survivor Bible Style!

Can you imagine what it would be like to be outnumbered 450 to 1? Think about having everyone in your whole school against you, and you'd be getting close. But Elijah didn't bat an eye. He didn't worry about the odds. Because he knew God was on his side. God is on our side, too, if we choose to worship him as Elijah did.

Toss the four numbered balls to different parts of the room. Bring the kids with the balls to the front one-by-one and ask these questions. Allow kids to get help from the group if they need it. After each correct answer, let kids drop their balls into a bag.

■ **What do you suppose the prophets of Baal were thinking as they prepared their altar? What about Elijah?**

■ **Why did Elijah pour water on his altar, even after Baal failed to send any fire?**

■ **After God sent fire to Elijah's sacrifice, many people stopped worshiping false gods and began to worship the one, true God. What "false gods" keep people from worshiping God today?**

■ **How can you turn away from those "false gods" this week?**

When this showdown started, most people didn't think Elijah would be the survivor. How could he win when he was only one man against so many? But this contest wasn't about the power of men. It was about God. Through the prophet Elijah, God showed the people of Israel that he is the one true God of the universe, and he alone deserved their worship.

There are people today who say there is no God. And, just like in Elijah's day, there are people who think it's fine to make up their own idea of god. But we know that our God, the God of the Bible, is the only true God and that Jesus is his Son. God answered when Elijah called, and he hears us when we call too. Today in your shepherd groups, you'll talk more about ways you can choose to follow the one, true God.

Dismiss kids to their shepherd groups.

Bible Verse
O LORD God Almighty, who is like you? You are mighty, O LORD, and your faithfulness surrounds you.
Psalm 89:8

Gather your small group and help kids find 1 Kings 18 in their Bibles.

The prophet Elijah lived in a time when few people believed in God. King Ahab and Queen Jezebel encouraged the people of Israel to worship idols. They were among the worst leaders Israel ever had. Elijah was God's messenger during this dark time. He made a bold move to show the people once and for all that God is God.

Have volunteers take turns reading 1 Kings 18:21–26, 29, 30, 33–36, 38, 39 aloud.

■ **Why do you think Elijah challenged the prophets of Baal to a showdown?**

■ **Do you know some people who don't believe in God? How can we help them believe?**

Pass out the "Fire on the Altar!" handout. **People in Bible times were used to offering sacrifices on an altar to worship God. They would place meat on top of an altar prepared with wood for the fire. Then they would light the fire. In today's story, the fire came from heaven. No matches, no lighters, just the power of God. And all the people saw God's power in an unforgettable way.**

Have kids cut and assemble the altar according to the instructions on the handout. Invite a volunteer to read the *"O LORD God Almighty, who is like you? You are mighty, O LORD and your faithfulness surrounds you" Psalm 89:8.*

Today in our prayer time, let's remember friends and relatives who don't believe in God. When I pause, you add their names, either silently or out loud. Dear Lord, you are incredible. You made the whole world and everything in it. We see your hand in everything you created and we feel your love in our hearts. Today we want to pray for people who don't have faith in you. Right now we remember (pause for kids to add names). Please hear our prayer, just as you heard Elijah's. In Jesus' name, amen.

Permission to photocopy this lesson page granted for local church use. Copyright © Cook Communications Ministries.
Printed in Pick Up 'n' Do Lessons on Survivor Bible Style!

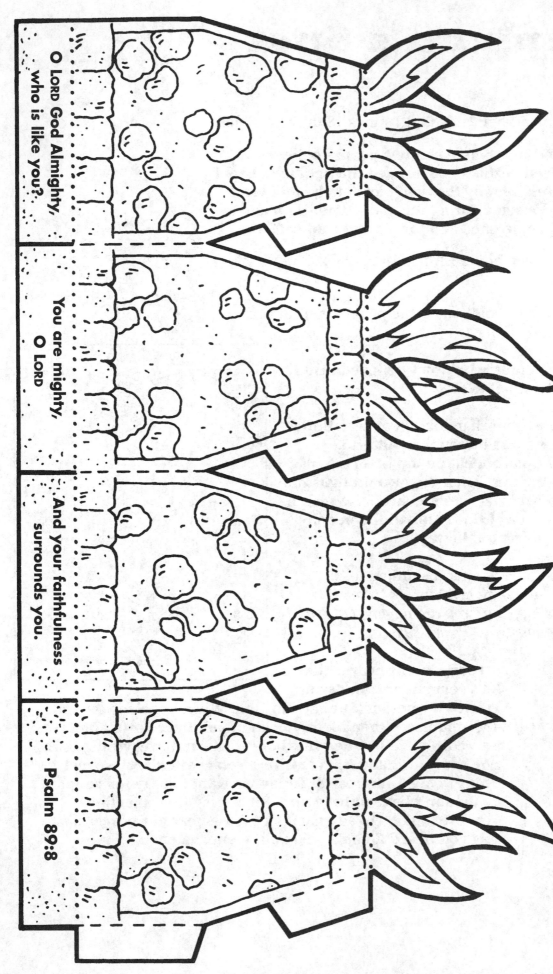

Fire on the Altar!

When Elijah prayed and God sent fire from heaven, everyone could see that our God is the one and only God. God still shows himself today in the mighty things he does in our lives. Make this fiery altar as a reminder that you serve our mighty, faithful God!

1. Cut out the altar on the solid lines. You'll find it easier to cut the flames by cutting from the tip down.
2. Fold the sides of the altar and the tabs. Put a little glue on the tabs and attach them to fasten the top of the altar together.
3. Bend the flames slightly forward.
4. Fold the bottom sections forward so you can read the verse as you turn the altar.

O Lord God Almighty, who is like you?

You are mighty, O Lord

And your faithfulness surrounds you.

Psalm 89:8

Permission to photocopy this handout granted for local church use. Copyright © Cook Communications Ministries.
Printed in Pick Up 'n' Do Lessons on Survivor Bible Style!

Because we believe in one true God, anything we make or build with our hands is not worthy of worship. It's fun to be creative. And we love making things. But we know from today's story that nothing made by people can be a substitute for our living God.

- Why do you think the people of Elijah's day spent time and prayer worshiping idols they could see and/or touch?

- Do people today worship idols? Why or why not?

Get List:
- ☐ erasers in all shapes, sizes and colors
- ☐ miscellaneous office supplies (Example: pencils, pushpins, paper clips, brass paper fasteners, rubber bands, thumbtacks, map tacks, binder clip wings, paper hole reinforcers)

The people in our story tried everything they could to get the Baal god to answer them and come to their rescue. The harder they tried, however, the sillier they looked. Baal could not answer them because it was not a living god. Baal was a man-made thing of wood and stone. Idols can not hear, see or love.

Our God, and the God of Elijah, is the one true living God. We can count on him at all times. His love for us is dependable and sure.

It doesn't take a lot of time or effort to make something that amuses us. Point out all the office supplies on the table. In a few minutes, you'll use these things to make little eraser critters. They're cute and fun! And it's a wonderful way to use the imagination God gave us. We're making cute figures for fun—much different than the idols in today's Bible story. We worship God, not things made with our hands.

Have students choose an eraser for the creature's body, then use various office supplies to complete their one-of-a-kind creations. Allow students plenty of time to finish their projects, then "parade" their creations around the table.

It's fun to make little creatures, but it would foolish and sinful to worship them. Our Bible verse reminds us that our worship is for God alone. Have a volunteer read Psalm 89:8: *"O LORD God Almighty, who is like you? You are mighty, O LORD, and your faithfulness surrounds you."*

The world we live in makes gods—some of stone and wood, others in the form of TVs, DVDs, computer games and other cool stuff. Don't waste your time putting faith in any of these. You will not be heard. We worship the one true God because he alone hears and cares and loves us.

Fold down the corners to start your paper airplane.

SPECIAL DELIVERY

TO

Worship God.

Today at church we learned how Elijah challenged the prophets of Baal and won, showing everyone that our God is the only true God.

◊ What important job did the prophet Elijah do for God's people?

False gods are full of empty "bubble" promises—here today and gone tomorrow! Fill a glass three-quarters full with cold water. Place a thin cotton cloth over the glass and hold it in place with a rubber band. Gently push down on the cloth until it touches the water. With your fingers still in place, turn the glass over. No spills! Pull the cloth tighter and watch the water (you guessed it!) bubble. Who is like our God? No other. Let his faithfulness fill you.

Bible Verse

O LORD God Almighty, who is like you? You are mighty, O LORD, and your faithfulness surrounds you.
Psalms 89:8

◊ Are there things in our lives that seem more important than God? How can we change that?

◊ When do you feel God's presence most—when you're praying, walking in the woods, singing a praise song?

Family FUN

Live It!

36   Permission to photocopy this handout granted for local church use. Copyright © Cook Communications Ministries.
Printed in Pick Up 'n' Do Lessons on Survivor Bible Style!

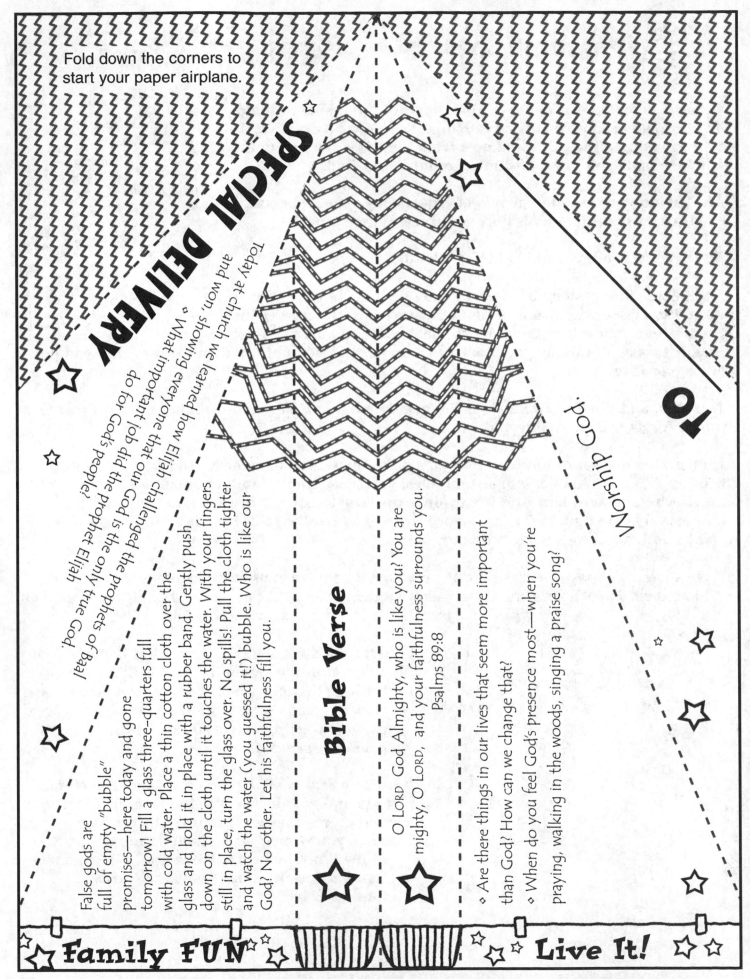

Prophet on the Run

Get Set
Option

LARGE GROUP ■ Greet kids and do a puppet skit. Schooner square dances—in a circle!—and learns that God speaks to us when we feel like giving up.

❏ large bird puppet ❏ puppeteer

Bible 4U! Instant Drama
1

LARGE GROUP ■ An angel cares for Elijah as he runs from Queen Jezebel; God speaks to Elijah and encourages him.

❏ 3 actors ❏ copies of pp. 40-41, Run, Prophet, Run! script ❏ 4 numbered balls
Optional: ❏ desert setting with tree and cave ❏ costumes for the Angel and Elijah
❏ water bottle ❏ bread ❏ paper balls

Shepherd's Spot
2

SMALL GROUP ■ Use the "God Whispers" handout to help kids learn the importance of taking time to listen to God.

❏ Bibles ❏ pencils ❏ scissors ❏ copies of p. 44, God Whispers ❏ copies of p. 46, Special Delivery

Workshop Wonders
Option

SMALL GROUP ■ Play a game where listening to quiet voices is the key.

❏ bag of treats ❏ blindfold

Bible Basis
God encourages Elijah.
1 Kings 19:2–15, 19

Learn It!
God speaks to us.

Live It!
Listen for God's voice.

Bible Verse
I will listen to what God the LORD will say; he promises peace to his people.
Psalm 85:8

Quick Takes

19:2 Jezebel sent a messenger to Elijah to say, "May the gods deal with me, be it ever so severely, if by this time tomorrow I do not make your life like that of one of them."
3 Elijah was afraid and ran for his life. When he came to Beersheba in Judah, he left his servant there,
4 while he himself went a day's journey into the desert. He came to a broom tree, sat down under it and prayed that he might die. "I have had enough, LORD," he said. "Take my life; I am no better than my ancestors."
5 Then he lay down under the tree and fell asleep. All at once an angel touched him and said, "Get up and eat."
6 He looked around, and there by his head was a cake of bread baked over hot coals, and a jar of water. He ate and drank and then lay down again.
7 The angel of the LORD came back a second time and touched him and said, "Get up and eat, for the journey is too much for you."
8 So he got up and ate and drank. Strengthened by that food, he traveled for forty days and forty nights until he reached Horeb, the mountain of God.
9 There he went into a cave and spent the night. And the word of the LORD came to him: "What are you doing here, Elijah?"
10 He replied, "I have been very zealous for the LORD God Almighty. The Israelites have rejected your covenant, broken down your altars, and put your prophets to death with the sword. I am the only one left, and now they are trying to kill me too."
11 The LORD said, "Go out and stand on the mountain in the presence of the LORD, for the LORD is about to pass by." Then a great and powerful wind tore the mountains apart and shattered the rocks before the LORD, but the LORD was not in the wind. After the wind there was an earthquake, but the LORD was not in the earthquake.
12 After the earthquake came a fire, but the LORD was not in the fire. And after the fire came a gentle whisper.
13 When Elijah heard it, he pulled his cloak over his face and went out and stood at the mouth of the cave. Then a voice said to him, "What are you doing here, Elijah?"
14 He replied, "I have been very zealous for the LORD God Almighty. The Israelites have rejected your covenant, broken down your altars, and put your prophets to death with the sword. I am the only one left, and now they are trying to kill me too."
15 The LORD said to him, "Go back the way you came...I reserve seven thousand in Israel—all whose knees have not bowed down to Baal and all whose mouths have not kissed him."
19 So Elijah went from there and found Elisha son of Shaphat...Elijah went up to him and threw his cloak around him.

Insights

In this story we see the very human side of Elijah. He boldly faced down hundreds of prophets of Baal on Mt. Carmel, and God's power won the day. But when a death threat came from vengeful Queen Jezebel, he tucked in his robe and ran for his life!

When God calls us to do things far beyond our own capability, we rise to the occasion with the assurance of his presence and power. But when it's over, we're spent, weary and vulnerable. So it was for Elijah. He sat down in the desert and begged to die.

Even the greatest prophets felt moments of overwhelming weakness and despair. To find their balance, they needed to get away and listen for the still, small voice of God. Depression is common among children today: circumstances in their families and on TV seem far out of control and hopelessness sets in. Use this lesson to teach kids that in our most desperate times of discouragement, we need to listen for the still, small voice of God. He will never desert us.

Option Get Set

Open with lively music, then greet the kids. **We cheer on the teams we care about. Go, team, go! God does the same for us. Even when we're tired and disappointed and try to hide from him. Schooner come and join us.** *Schooner pops up.*

Schooner: *(ruffles feathers)* I've had enough!

Leader: What's up?

Schooner: How many times can you try before just giving up?

Leader: *(ponders a bit)* I don't have an answer for that, Schooner.

Schooner: I do. Four!

Leader: Why don't you tell us the whole story?

Schooner: I've tried four times to learn the basic moves in square dancing but I just can't do it.

Leader: Square dancing?

Schooner: A bunch of us birds go out to Parrot Square and fly in circles.

Leader: *(shakes head)* What!?!

Schooner: We go out to Parrot Square and fly in circles.

Leader: You fly circles in the Square?

Schooner: Sometimes we line dance, too.

Leader: *(scratches head)* Squares. Circles. Lines. My head hurts!

Schooner: No kidding! That's why I want to give up.

Leader: The prophet in today's story felt the same way.

Schooner: You mean he couldn't learn to square dance?

Leader: No.

Schooner: He couldn't fly in circles?

Leader: No.

Schooner: Then what was his problem, boss?

Leader: Elijah was God's faithful prophet. But he had had enough. Enough of false prophets and evil people and one mean queen.

Schooner: So?

Leader: So he ran away into the desert.

Schooner: Not my favorite vacation spot.

Leader: Good point. He almost died. But God sent an angel to take care of him.

Schooner: Room service!

Leader: Later on in the story Prophet Elijah heard something.

Schooner: A bird?

Leader: No.

Schooner: A plane?

Leader: No.

Schooner: Superman?

Leader: Stay focused, Schooner.

Schooner: Right, boss.

Leader: God spoke words of comfort to our tired and fed up Elijah.

Schooner: I didn't know God had a mouth!

Leader: God spoke to Elijah in a whisper.

Schooner: When I think of God I think of thunder and lightning and stuff. Are you sure God spoke in a whisper?

Leader: Look up 1 Kings 19 in your Bible. It's all there.

Schooner: *(ponders)* The Bible is God's Holy Word,

Leader: Yes.

Schooner: So what you say has to be true.

Leader: Yes again.

Schooner: Boss?

Leader: Yes?

Schooner: How do we know when God speaks to us? Will it be a whisper too?

Leader: I don't know, Schooner.

Schooner: Well, how are we supposed to know?

Leader: We live by faith. In faith I believe we'll know his voice when we hear it.

Schooner: I get it.

Leader: Let's listen for God's voice.

Schooner: I'm all ears.

Leader: Then let's move on to Bible 4U!

Permission to photocopy this script granted for local church use. Copyright © Cook Communications Ministries. Printed in Pick Up 'n' Do Lessons on Survivor Bible Style!

Welcome back to Bible 4U!. The last time we were together, we heard how Elijah showed the prophets of Baal a thing or two. After dumping water all over his offering, Elijah prayed for fire and fire came. Then, after three years of drought, God sent rain. First a little tiny cloud appeared, then bigger, darker clouds filled the sky.

Instant Prep
Before class, ask two older kids to play the roles of Elijah and the Lord. Ask a younger child to play the role of the angel. Give the angel sheets of paper with "Day 1," through "Day 40." Give all three kids copies of the script below.

King Ahab and Queen Jezebel should have been happy that it was finally raining after three long years. Instead, they were furious that Elijah had humiliated the prophets of Baal. Jezebel threatened to kill Elijah the very next day!

for Overachievers
Dress Elijah and the Angel in costumes. Have the voice of the Lord off stage. Create a desert setting with a tree and a cave where Elijah rests. Have the angel set out bread and water for Elijah to eat. Have extras throw paper wad "rocks" at Elijah when the mountain shakes.

What would you do if you heard someone was going to try to kill you tomorrow? Would you wait until tomorrow, or would you start running right now? Well, that's just what Elijah did. He packed up his things and he ran for his life. He should be passing this way soon.

Run, Prophet, Run!
Based on 1 Kings 19

Elijah tiptoes in and begins packing things into a knapsack.

Elijah: Sssh! Don't let Queen Jezebel know I'm here. She's out to get me… Oh, by the way, let me introduce myself. Name's Elijah, and I'm…well… *(looks around)* a prophet. Sssh! Jezebel hates prophets—especially God's prophets. She's already killed most of them, and she'd love to kill me, too. *(Looks around, startled, and gasps.)* I've got to get away from here, or my goose is cooked!

Elijah hastily grabs his things and exits, then re-enters, running across the room several times.

Elijah: Got to get away…Jezebel…killing prophets…run! *(Runs faster, then begins to breathe heavily and slow down.)* Get away…hot desert…can't…make it… *(Falls over.)* Oh, it's just no use! No matter where I go, she'll find me. Lord, I've had enough. I'm ready to go. Take my life.

Elijah lies down and falls asleep, then begins to snore. An angel enters and taps Elijah on the shoulder. He turns over and keeps snoring. The angel shakes him.

Angel: Elijah!

Elijah: What…huh…who are you? *(Rubs eyes.)* Am I dead?

Angel shakes his head and points to food and drink. If you aren't using props, have Elijah pretend to eat and drink.

Angel: Get up and eat. *(Angel leaves.)*

Elijah: *(rubbing eyes again)* Fresh, hot bread? A full jar of water? I must be dreaming. But what a dream! *(Eats and drinks, then rubs tummy.)* Aah! And now for a little afternoon nap. *(Lies down to sleep.)*

Angel re-enters, starts to tap Elijah, then shakes his head and goes right to shaking Elijah this time. Elijah wakes up.

Angel: Eat! Eat! You've got a long ways to go yet.

Elijah hesitates, then eats greedily. Elijah gets up, collects his things and starts to walk, whistling or humming as he goes.

Elijah: I'm feeling much better. I bet I could walk for 40 days.

Angel holds up calendar pages: Day 1, 2, 3, 4, 5, Day 10, 20, 30, 39, Day 40.

Elijah: Yep. 40 days. I think I need to get my bearings. *(Looks around.)* Wow—this is Mount Horeb. This is the mountain where God talked to Moses! If anyplace is safe, it's Mount Horeb. Now…somewhere around here there should be a little…here it is—a little cave. Good place to spend the night.

Lord: Elijah.

Elijah: *(to kids)* Did you hear that? It sounded like…

Lord: Elijah!

Elijah: Yep, it's the Lord all right! Yes, Lord?

Lord: Elijah, what are you doing here?

Elijah: Well…er…um…You see, Lord, it's like this. You know I love being your prophet. But that's just it, you see…I like my life. The people of Israel—they don't like it so much. They've been taking out prophets with swords one-by-one, and I think I'm next. So that's why I'm here. Just trying to stay alive. It feels like I'm the only one who's still loyal to you.

Lord: Go out. Stand on the mountain in front of me. I am going to pass by.

Elijah: *(Stepping forward)* Okay, here I go. Whoa, it's getting windy all of a sudden. Ooh…ouch! *(Rubs head.)* I didn't see any signs about rockslides. *(Starts to shake.)* Oh great, now there's also an earthquake…Lord…is that you? *(Jumps back.)* Youch! Fire! Hot, hot, hot! Lord, did you send this…fire…hey, it's gone. And the earthquake stopped, too. Shh… *(Covers face and whispers.)* Lord, is that you? That still, small voice? It's you, isn't it? I'm listening.

Lord: Elijah, what are you doing here?

Elijah: You know I've been very faithful to you. But no one else is following your ways. And they're trying to kill me.

Lord: Go back the way you came. On the way, anoint Hazael king over Aram. Anoint Jehu king over Israel. Anoint Elisha to be the next prophet after you. When it's all said and done, 7,000 people in Israel will remain my faithful followers.

Elijah: *(to himself)* Hmmm…7,000. And a new prophet, too. I can do that.

Elijah exits.

Permission to photocopy this script granted for local church use. Copyright © Cook Communications Ministries.
Printed in Pick Up 'n' Do Lessons on Survivor Bible Style!

Elijah survived his discouraging time and the evil queen didn't get him! Elijah knew God was powerful—after all, God had just answered his prayer and set fire to a watery altar. So when Elijah was told to wait for God's voice, he was expecting God to speak in the strong wind, the earthquake or the fire. Elijah was probably surprised to hear God speaking in the still, small voice. But that little voice definitely got Elijah's attention. He listened carefully to God's instructions, and went right away to do what God asked. And as he listened to God, he realized that maybe things weren't as bad as they seemed—7,000 people would still choose to follow God.

Sometimes God speaks in surprising ways. Let's talk more about listening for God's voice.

Toss the four numbered balls to different parts of the room. Bring the kids with the balls to the front one-by-one and ask these questions. Allow kids to get help from the group if they need it. After each correct answer, let kids drop their balls into a bag.

■ **You're Elijah. You've passed out in the desert from heat exhaustion. When you wake up you see an angel offering you food. What's your first thought?**

■ **Why do you think God spoke in a still, small voice instead of in the wind, the earthquake or the fire?**

■ **God was with Elijah when he was afraid. Do you remember a time when you were afraid but you knew God was with you? Tell about it.**

■ **In what unexpected ways do people hear from God today?**

God really does speak to us, but we have to be listening to hear it. Sometimes God speaks through the Bible—we can read a new story or verse and learn something that helps us follow God. If we memorize parts of God's Word, God can "speak" by bringing those verses to mind when we need them. God can also speak to us through parents, teachers and caring friends who love us and want to help us follow God.

Today in your shepherd groups, you'll talk more about what it means to listen for God's voice.

Dismiss kids to their shepherd groups.

Bible Verse
I will listen to what God the LORD will say; he promises peace to his people.
Psalm 85:8

Gather your small group and help kids find 1 Kings 19 in their Bibles.

Wow—this is a different Elijah than we saw before! Who remembers what Elijah did on Mt. Carmel? (Defeated 450 prophets of Baal.) **After that great victory, he was definitely on mean Queen Jezebel's bad list. In fact, she promised to kill him. Elijah didn't wait around to find out if she could do it—he decided it was time to head for the hills!**

Have volunteers take turns reading 1 Kings 19:2–15, 19 aloud.

◼ **Why do you think Elijah was so strong and courageous one day, and scared to death the next day?**

◼ **How does it make you feel to know that a great prophet of God would want to run away and give up?**

Prophets were God's messengers, but they were people too. And people get worn out, scared and discouraged. That's why we all need to take time to listen to God.

Pass out the "God Whispers" handout. Have kids cut out and assemble the 3D cave. **This is like the cave where Elijah rested.** Ask a volunteer to read the verse inside the cave: *"I will listen to what God the LORD will say; he promises peace to his people." Psalm 85:8.*

Elijah needed "listening to God time." So do you. So do I.

◼ **When is a good time for you to listen to God?**

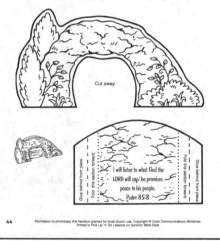

Did you know that listening is an important part of praying? When we pray, we don't need to do all the talking. Sometimes we just need to be quiet and listen for God's voice. It may feel funny at first. You can quiet your heart by humming a little praise song. Let's take a little listening time as we pray today. Let kids share their concerns, then close with prayer. **Dear Lord, sometimes we feel like Elijah—we get tired and confused and want to give up. When that happens, remind us to listen for your still, small voice. We want to listen to you right now.** Pause for just a few moments. **Thank you for giving us your peace. In Jesus' name, amen.**

Permission to photocopy this lesson page granted for local church use. Copyright © Cook Communications Ministries.
Printed in Pick Up 'n' Do Lessons on Survivor Bible Style!

God Whispers

Full of doubt and fear, Elijah hid in a cave. There God spoke to him. Create a 3-D listening cave where you can listen to what God has to say to you!

1. Cut out the two cave pieces.
2. Cut away the door to the cave.
3. Fold the back panel on the dotted lines so the Bible Verse is set back.
4. Glue the sides to the back of the front piece so the verse shows through the door.

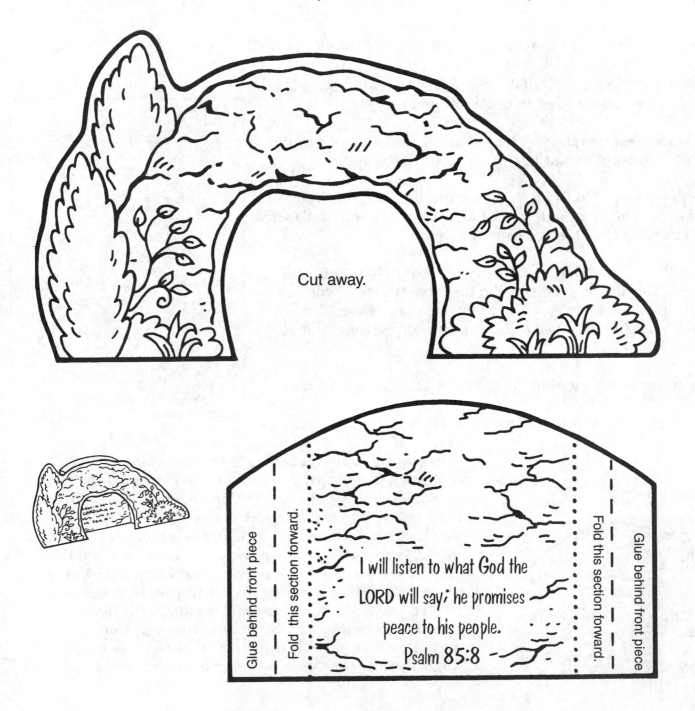

Cut away.

Glue behind front piece

Fold this section forward.

I will listen to what God the LORD will say; he promises peace to his people. — Psalm 85:8 —

Fold this section forward.

Glue behind front piece

Permission to photocopy this handout granted for local church use. Copyright © Cook Communications Ministries.
Printed in Pick Up 'n' Do Lessons on Survivor Bible Style

Workshop Wonders

Get List:
- ☐ blindfold
- ☐ treats

Once your kids gather, clap your hands twice to draw attention to you. Then whisper the following to your class. (Be sure to speak softly and slowly, forming the words carefully.) **God told Elijah to stand on the mountain and wait for him to pass by. He wasn't in the wind, earthquake, or the fire. How did God talk to Elijah? A whisper. You have to listen really carefully when someone whispers. When God spoke to Elijah, Elijah somehow recognized God's voice. He then listened carefully to what God had to say to him. Turn to your neighbor and whisper today's Bible verse, Psalm 85:8. Shhh!** Pause for kids to whisper to one another. *"I will listen to what God the LORD will say; he promises peace to his people." Psalm 85:8.*

■ **Do you think God recognizes your voice apart from the millions of other voices in the world? Why or why not?**

■ **What do you think God might say to you?**

With all the noise around us, we barely have time to listen for God's quiet voice. Let's see what that's like. I need someone to volunteer to leave the room. When the volunteer is out of earshot, explain the game to the rest of the kids.

I have this bag of treats. Where should I hide it for our volunteer to find? Hide the treats. **When** (name) **returns,** (he, she) **will be wearing a blindfold. You'll guide** (him, her) **to the treat by saying "hot" or "cold." The trick is, half of you are going to say the wrong thing. When** (name) **gets close to the treat, you'll shout, "Cold, cold, cold!" The rest of you will guide** (name) **correctly, but you'll do it in very soft voices so** (he, she) **will really have to listen to hear you—especially since the rest of the class is giving wrong instructions very loudly!**

Have the kids form two groups. Then bring your blindfolded volunteer back into the room. **You've got an important job: find the bag of treats everyone is going to share. Listen for instructions from your classmates. They'll tell you whether you're hot or cold.** Play until the volunteer finds the treats, even though it may take some patience. Enjoy the treats while you discuss the experience.

■ **What was it like to hear the wrong directions being shouted?**

■ **What keeps us from hearing the voice of God today?**

God wants us to listen for his voice. Sometimes we listen with our eyes, by reading the words of the Bible. Sometimes we hear God's voice through wise parents and teachers. And sometimes he speaks in our hearts when everything is still at night. What is God saying to you? Stop, rest and listen.

Permission to photocopy this lesson page granted for local church use. Copyright © Cook Communications Ministries.
Printed in Pick Up 'n' Do Lessons on Survivor Bible Style!

Fold down the corners to start your paper airplane.

SPECIAL DELIVERY

TO

Worship God!

Today at church we learned that when Elijah was afraid, God spoke to him in a quiet voice.

• Why did a fearful Elijah run into the wilderness? *(Jezebel promised to kill him.)*
• Who tended to Elijah's needs when he was exhausted and lonely? *(God's angel.)*

Make easy peanut butter cookies —"earmarked" just for you! The treats will remind you to open your ears and heart and be ready to listen for God's voice. Mix 1 cup peanut butter with 1 cup sugar and 1 egg. Drop by spoonfuls onto a greased baking tray. Use a sugar-dipped fork to make the cookies ear-shaped, then press a cross design into each one. Bake cookies in a 350° oven for eight minutes.

Bible Verse

I will listen to what God the LORD will say; he promises peace to his people.
Psalms 85:8

◊ Why do you think that God chose to speak to Elijah in a quiet whisper instead of the roar of a burning fire?
◊ When and where can you listen for God's voice?
◊ What things get in the way of listening to what God has to say?

☆ Family FUN ☆   Live It!

Permission to photocopy this handout granted for local church use. Copyright © Cook Communications Ministries.
Printed in Pick Up 'n' Do Lessons on Survivor Bible Style!

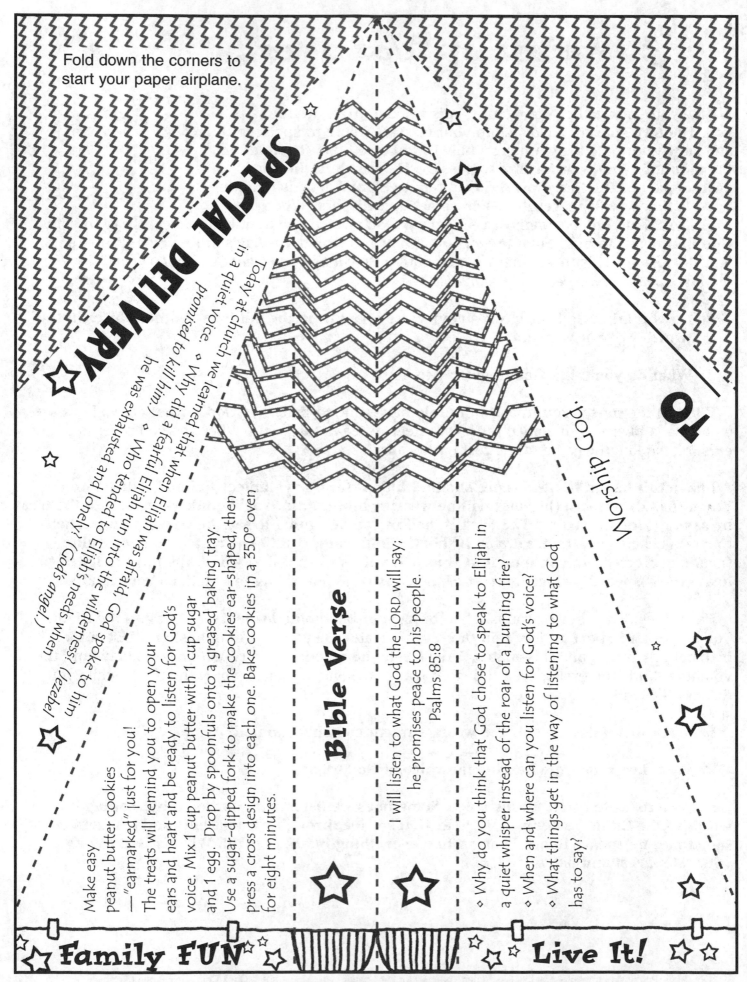

Who's Calling?

Option

Get Set

LARGE GROUP ■ Greet kids and do a puppet skit. Cross paths with Schooner as he answers God's call to tell others about Jesus.

❑ large bird puppet ❑ puppeteer

1

Bible 4U! Instant Drama

LARGE GROUP ■ Isaiah sees God in the temple and answers God's call.

❑ 4 actors ❑ copies of pp. 50-51, God's Call script ❑ 4 numbered balls
Optional: ❑ two angel costumes, one simple prophet costume ❑ rolling office chair
❑ confetti or bubbles ❑ ball of red paper

2

Shepherd's Spot

SMALL GROUP ■ Use the "Share the Light" handout to encourage kids to speak to others about God's love.

❑ Bibles ❑ pencils ❑ scissors ❑ copies of p. 54, Share the Light ❑ copies of p. 56, Special Delivery

Option

Workshop Wonders

SMALL GROUP ■ Make a googly-eyed prophet finger puppet and use it to practice telling others about God.

❑ Bible ❑ waxed paper ❑ work gloves ❑ scraps of dark fabric ❑ Spanish moss
❑ fabric glue or hot glue (hot glue only with extra adult help) ❑ wiggly eyes
Optional: ❑ pencils

Bible Basis
Isaiah answers God's call.
Isaiah 6:1–8; 9:1–6

Learn It!
God calls people to speak for him.

Live It!
Share the light of God's love.

Bible Verse
I heard the voice of the LORD saying, "Whom shall I send? And who will go for us?" And I said, "Here am I. Send me!"
Isaiah 6:8

Quick Takes

Isaiah 6:1–8; 9:1–6

6:1 In the year that King Uzziah died, I saw the Lord seated on a throne, high and exalted, and the train of his robe filled the temple.
2 Above him were seraphs, each with six wings: With two wings they covered their faces, with two they covered their feet, and with two they were flying.
3 And they were calling to one another: "Holy, holy, holy is the LORD Almighty; the whole earth is full of his glory."
4 At the sound of their voices the door posts and thresholds shook and the temple was filled with smoke.
5 "Woe to me!" I cried. "I am ruined! For I am a man of unclean lips, and I live among a people of unclean lips, and my eyes have seen the King, the LORD Almighty."
6 Then one of the seraphs flew to me with a live coal in his hand, which he had taken with tongs from the altar.
7 With it he touched my mouth and said, "See, this has touched your lips; your guilt is taken away and your sin atoned for."
8 Then I heard the voice of the Lord saying, "Whom shall I send? And who will go for us?" And I said, "Here am I. Send me!"

9:1 Nevertheless, there will be no more gloom for those who were in distress. In the past he humbled the land of Zebulun and the land of Naphtali, but in the future he will honor Galilee of the Gentiles, by the way of the sea, along the Jordan—
2 The people walking in darkness have seen a great light; on those living in the land of the shadow of death a light has dawned.
3 You have enlarged the nation and increased their joy; they rejoice before you as people rejoice at the harvest, as men rejoice when dividing the plunder.
4 For as in the day of Midian's defeat, you have shattered the yoke that burdens them, the bar across their shoulders, the rod of their oppressor.
5 Every warrior's boot used in battle and every garment rolled in blood will be destined for burning, will be fuel for the fire.
6 For to us a child is born, to us a son is given, and the government will be on his shoulders. And he will be called Wonderful Counselor, Mighty God, Everlasting Father, Prince of Peace.

Insights

What happens when a mere man encounters almighty God?

Isaiah must have felt fortunate to survive. Even though Isaiah was a holy man of God, he trembled at the realization of his sin in comparison to God's holiness. God sent the angel with a hot coal to cleanse Isaiah's guilt and sin. When the sight of God filled Isaiah with terror, God reached out in compassion and forgiveness. How like God!

God spoke to Isaiah at a critical time in the history of Judah. Threatened by an alliance from the north, King Ahaz took gold and silver from the temple and sent it to appease Assyria. But soon Judah would be invaded, Jerusalem and its temple destroyed, and the people deported. In this time of imminent terror, God sent Isaiah with the message that the exile would not last forever—in time God would bring his people back.

God called Isaiah to speak of hope in a dark time when the nation was threatened by overwhelming forces of evil. God needs people to speak the same message of hope today. Use this lesson to encourage kids to bring God's hope to the world.

Before your talk, borrow a carpet square from your church nursery. Be sure kids see you place it at your feet. Open with lively music, then greet your group. **God wants us to speak to others with his words in our heart. Today we'll hear about telling others about the love and hope God offers. Schooner, come and join our handsome group.** *Schooner pops up.*

Schooner: Knock. Knock.

Leader: I'm game! Who's there?

Schooner: Pizza.

Leader: Pizza who?

Schooner: I see you got a new "pizza" carpet for our talk today!

Leader: Very clever, Schooner.

Schooner: Clever Schooner, clever Schooner. *Squawk!*

Leader: Let's talk today about telling others about Jesus.

Schooner: How about we do it with a cheer?

Leader: We could do that.

Schooner: *(looks to the group)* Everyone join in. Give me a "G."

Leader and kids: "G"

Schooner: Give me an "E."

Leader: "E." Slow down, Schooner. Jesus begins with the letter "J" not "G."

Schooner: Oops! I'm always getting those two mixed up. Give me a "J."

Leader and kids: "J."

Schooner: Give me a "J-E-S-U-S."

Leader and kids: "J-E-S-U-S."

Schooner: What's that spell?

Leader and kids: Jesus!

Schooner: *(very proud of himself) Squawk!* Clever bird, clever kids!

Leader: *(picks up the carpet square)* Let's say, this is the welcome mat outside your front door at home.

Schooner: I have one of those!

Leader: Good.

Schooner: But mine says, "Parrot Crossing." 'Cause I'm a parrot.

Leader: I figured that out, friend.

Schooner: My mat has flowers.

Leader: Can we hurry this along?

Schooner: *(continues)* And it's made from crushed walnuts and cherry pits.

Leader: *(sighs)* As I was saying, let's pretend that this is the welcome mat that greets friends and visitors to your door.

Schooner: I'm with you, boss.

Leader: Your doorbell suddenly rings.

Schooner: Nicki-nicki-nicki-noo! Nicki-nicki-nicki-noo!

Leader: Let me guess. That's the sound of your doorbell.

Schooner: Got a certain ring to it doesn't it?

Leader: Let's pretend it's the pizza delivery person.

Schooner: If it's an extra large with pineapple and anchovies, it's mine.

Leader: My question: how eager are you to run to the door and say, Here am I! Here am I!

Schooner: Very eager.

Leader: With just as much eagerness, God wants us to speak to others about him.

Schooner: Is there a Bible verse that will help us remember that, boss?

Leader: Why, of course. There's a whole story, in fact.

Schooner: Does it have a parrot in it?

Leader: Nope, it has a prophet. His name was Isaiah.

Schooner: I have a second cousin named Isaiah. He doesn't talk much, though.

Leader: Well, the Isaiah in our story had plenty to say. And it came straight from God.

Schooner: Let's hear it, then!

Leader: Bible 4U! up next.

1 Bible 4U!

Isaiah was God's prophet. Today's story tells us how God called him into service to speak of hope during a time when the nation was threatened by evil forces.

We're going to need a lot of help to make this story really stand out. We need a special effects team that will transform this story into an action-packed experience. First I need two earth-shaking personalities. (Pick two.) Now we need two smoke-makers. (Pick two.) They'll blow bubbles to represent smoke.

Instant Prep

Select an excellent reader to be Isaiah, or play him yourself. Pick two Seraphs and one person to be the voice of the Lord offstage. Have kids blow bubbles (or tear paper) to make confetti "smoke." Recruit five special effects people. Give each a copy of God's call.

for Overachievers

Have drama team prepare the story. Dress Isaiah in Bible costume. Two seraphs have white robes, hats and feet bands with paper wings or white crepe paper streamers. Prepare a backdrop with pillars that suggests the temple. Rehearse the special effects with your crew.

Next, we need one who can give an on-again, off-again performance. (Pick one.) He/she will turn the lights off and on repeatedly, to give an electrifying affect.

Listen up! On Isaiah's cue, each of you will stomp your feet to give us the thunderous sound of earth shaking.

Are you ready for the action? Here comes Isaiah now!

God's Call
Based on Isaiah 6:1–8; 9:1–6

Isaiah: Greetings, my name is Isaiah. I am a prophet of God. God speaks to me and uses me to tell his people what he wants them to know. Sometimes, I tell them what they have been doing wrong. Sometimes, I tell them how to do better. I can even see things that haven't happened yet! God tells me with words or with a vision. That's like a dream, only I am awake.

Let me tell you about one of my most memorable visions. It was the time I answered God's call. I had gone into the temple to pray. I wasn't expecting anything more than my usual prayer time. Suddenly, I saw movement above me. When I looked I saw God seated on his throne. That's right— God himself. I was terrified! I'll try to tell you what it was like.

Extras roll in an office chair. Two helpers sit on floor beside the chair. One helper is stationed at the lights. Two helpers with bubbles or confetti kneel on either side of the stage.

Isaiah: In the year King Uzziah died, I saw the Lord seated on a throne, high and exalted, his robe filling the temple. Above him were seraphs each with six wings. Seraphs are angels. They had two wings that covered their faces, two that covered their feet, and two to fly with.

Seraphs enter from opposite sides. They walk in figure eight pattern up stage, behind Isaiah, flapping arms slowly.

Isaiah: They were calling…

Seraphs: Holy, holy, holy,

Isaiah: At the sound of their voices the thresholds and doorposts shook and the temple was filled with smoke.

Helpers shake the chair, flick the lights and blow bubbles or confetti "smoke." Signal the audience to stomp their feet.

Seraphs: Holy, holy, holy, is the Lord Almighty. The whole earth is full of his glory.

Helpers stop and exit.

Isaiah: Woe is me! I am ruined! For I am a man of unclean lips, among a people of unclean lips, and my eyes have seen the King, the Lord God Almighty!

Seraph One: *(touches a ball of red paper to Isaiah's mouth)* This hot coal has touched your lips. Your guilt is taken away. *(exits)*

Isaiah: Then I heard the voice of the Lord saying,

Lord: *(speaks offstage into bucket or large cup, in deep voice)* Whom shall I send? Who will go for us?

Isaiah: *(stands)* Here am I, Lord! Send me. *(pauses and steps forward)* Since that day I have spent my whole life telling, telling and telling, all that God wanted his people to know. I've brought the light of God's love into a dark world. Here is the most important message I gave to God's people. See if you can guess who it is talking about.

Seraphs One and Two enter and read to the audience.

Seraph One: The people walking in darkness have seen a light.

Seraph Two: For those in the shadow of death, the light has dawned.

Seraph One: You have made a nation bigger and they are rejoicing!

Seraph Two: For you shattered that big burden and heavy bar from their shoulders.

Seraph One: For unto us a child is born, to us a son is given.

Seraph Two: And the government shall be upon his shoulders.

Isaiah, Seraph One and Two: And He shall be called Wonderful Counselor, Mighty God, Everlasting Father, Prince of Peace!

Seraphs exit.

Isaiah: God spoke these words, they are about the one who was to come. You know him as Jesus. God wants everyone to know him, for in Jesus there is light and hope. He is the light of the world, and you are his messengers. Now go—tell!

Isaiah exits.

Permission to photocopy this script granted for local church use. Copyright © Cook Communications Ministries.
Printed in Pick Up 'n' Do Lessons on Survivor Bible Style!

When God called, Isaiah said "Here am I. Send me!" He didn't hesitate or try to get out of it. God is calling us too. When Jesus went into heaven he said, "Go into all the world and preach the gospel." The light that God spoke of needs to be spread throughout the world. We have good news of God's love that people everywhere need to hear.

Toss the four numbered balls to different parts of the room. Bring kids with the balls to the front one-by-one and ask these questions. Allow kids to get help from the group if they need it. After each correct answer, let kids drop their balls into a bag.

■ **How did Isaiah feel when he saw God? Why did he feel that way?**

■ **What did God ask Isaiah to do? Why was that important?**

■ **What is the great light Isaiah told about?**

■ **What's the most important thing people need to hear about God today?**

Isaiah had quite a surprising experience when he saw God in the temple. I'm not sure he expected to survive. But he did—and he went on to spread God's Word to everyone who would listen. God's people were facing a terrible situation. Powerful enemies were coming. Their country would be destroyed and they would be sent off to live in a different place. God's people desperately needed to hear God's words of love and hope, and of the light he would send into the world.

People need to hear about the hope God offers today. And you're just the ones to spread the word! Today in your shepherd groups, you'll get to learn what it means to spread the light of God's love.

Dismiss kids to their shepherd groups.

Bible Verse

I heard the voice of the LORD saying, "Whom shall I send? And who will go for us?" And I said, 'Here am I. Send me!'"
Isaiah 6:8

2 Shepherd's Spot

Gather your small group and help kids find Isaiah 6:1–8; 9:1–6 in their Bibles.

Isaiah lived in a time when God's people were scared. Enemies to the north had formed an alliance and they were ready to attack. The people knew their country would be destroyed. If they ever needed to hear from God, this was the time. That's why God called a very special messenger.

Have volunteers take turns reading Isaiah 6:1–8; 9:1–6 aloud.

■ **What kind of message did Isaiah give the people?**

■ **If you were going to spread a message of love and hope from God, what would you say?**

Pass out the "Share the Light" handout. Have kids cut out and assemble the votive candle ring according to the instructions on the handout.

Have a volunteer read Isaiah 6:8 from the handout: *"I heard the voice of the Lord saying, 'Whom shall I send? And who will go for us?' And I said, 'Here am I. Send me!'"*

■ **Where did God send Isaiah? Where does God send us?**

When you take this home, ask your parents to place this ring around a votive candle that's in a glass or metal holder. When they light the candle, the glow will come through candle ring.

■ **In what ways is our world a dark place?**

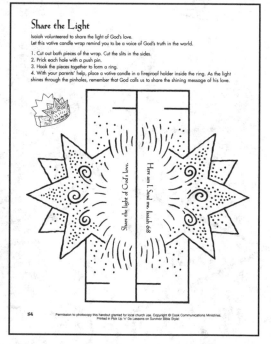

Share the Light

Isaiah volunteered to share the light of God's love.
Let this votive candle wrap remind you to be a voice of God's truth in the world.

1. Cut out both pieces of the wrap. Cut the slits in the sides.
2. Prick each hole with a push pin.
3. Hook the pieces together to form a ring.
4. With your parents' help, place a votive candle in a fireproof holder inside the ring. As the light shines through the pinholes, remember that God calls us to share the shining message of his love.

Share the light of God's love.
Here am I. Send me. Isaiah 6:8

54   Permission to photocopy this handout granted for local church use. Copyright © Cook Communications Ministries. Printed in Pick Up 'n' Do Lessons on Survivor Bible Style!

■ **How can you bring light and hope to people who don't know about God?**

Share the light of God's love.

God calls us to be his messengers. Isaiah was a very special messenger, but God might use you to speak to someone who has no one else to tell them about God's love. Let's pray for ourselves and for people who need to hear about the hope and light God's love can bring to dark places. Dear Lord, we may never see you like Isaiah did. But we offer ourselves as messengers of your word. Help us share your message of light and love with people who are in darkness. We especially pray for (pause for kids to mention names). Give us your words, we pray. In Jesus' name, amen.

Permission to photocopy this lesson page granted for local church use. Copyright © Cook Communications Ministries.
Printed in Pick Up 'n' Do Lessons on Survivor Bible Style!

Share the Light

Isaiah volunteered to share the light of God's love.
Let this votive candle wrap remind you to be a voice of God's truth in the world.

1. Cut out both pieces of the wrap. Cut the slits in the sides.
2. Prick each hole with a push pin.
3. Hook the pieces together to form a ring.
4. With your parents' help, place a votive candle in a fireproof holder inside the ring. As the light shines through the pinholes, remember that God calls us to share the shining message of his love.

Share the light of God's love.

Here am I. Send me. Isaiah 6:8

Permission to photocopy this handout granted for local church use. Copyright © Cook Communications Ministries.
Printed in Pick Up 'n' Do Lessons on Survivor Bible Style!

Workshop Wonders

Make a sample finger puppet before class.

When Isaiah saw God in the temple, he was shaking in his sandals. Even though he was a man who studied scripture and followed God, he knew he wasn't worthy to be in God's holy presence. So God sent an angel to put a hot coal on his lips—a sign that God forgave his sins. Then God gave Isaiah a job. Who remember what that was? Pause as kids respond. **Good! He could go and tell others God's message of love and hope.**

Let's make a little prophet of our own who can't wait to bring God's light to a dark world.

Have reliable older kids cut the fingers and thumbs from work gloves. Ask a second group to cut scraps of dark fabric into triangles that are approximately nine inches on the longer edge. (You may want to prepare a couple of triangle templates for them to work with.) Have kids distribute their cut materials to their classmates.

Get List:
- ❑ Bible
- ❑ waxed paper
- ❑ scissors
- ❑ work gloves
- ❑ scraps of dark fabric
- ❑ Spanish moss
- ❑ small wiggly eyes
- ❑ fabric glue or hot glue (hot glue only with extra adult help)

Optional
- ❑ pencils

Show your sample puppet, then lead kids through these steps to assemble their own.

1. Stuff the glove finger with waxed paper to make a firm working surface.
2. Glue on wiggly eyes.
3. Fold the edge of a fabric triangle back and glue it around the neck like a cloak. Overlap it slightly in front and glue it together.
4. Crumple and glue on bits of Spanish moss for hair and a beard. This step takes a bit of patience. Encourage kids who are quick to finish to help others glue on the hair and beard.
5. When the glue is dry, give the puppet a haircut to make the hair and beard a realistic shape.

As soon as the glue is dry, you can place your prophet puppet on a pencil or on your index finger.

■ **What would your prophet have to say about God's love? Practice sharing with your classmates.**

Permission to photocopy this lesson page granted for local church use. Copyright © Cook Communications Ministries.
Printed in Pick Up 'n' Do Lessons on Survivor Bible Style!

Fold down the corners to start your paper airplane.

SPECIAL DELIVERY

TO

Tell others about Jesus.

Today at church we learned that God called Isaiah to give his people a message of love and hope. "Ouch! Why did the angel touch Isaiah's lips with hot coal?" (His past wrongs were forgiven. His love free to do God's work.) Isaiah was free to do God's work.

Unless we speak out for Jesus we keep a treasure all to ourselves. Form a sitting game circle with your friends and stand in the middle. The game circle will secretly pass a bag of treats behind their backs from one to another. Try to guess the person with the treasure—then speak out! When you think you have the right player point and shout, Stop! If you guess right everyone must rise and shout, "Spread the news: God loves you!" Then share the treats. If not, switch places and continue play.

Bible Verse

I heard the voice of the Lord saying, "Whom shall I send? And who will go for us?" And I said, "Here am I. Send me! Isaiah 6:8

◊ What does an Old Testament story about an old prophet have to do with the way we live today?

◊ How do we know when it's a good time to tell someone about God?

◊ Can you think of someone who is in a "dark place" right now? How can we share the light of God's love?

☆ **Family FUN** ☆

Live It!

Permission to photocopy this handout granted for local church use. Copyright © Cook Communications Ministries.
Printed in Pick Up 'n' Do Lessons on Survivor Bible Style!

Hezekiah in a Hot Spot

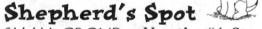

Option — Get Set

LARGE GROUP ■ Greet kids and do a puppet skit. Schooner hears of a one-of-a-kind king who calls to God for help.

❏ large bird puppet   ❏ puppeteer

1 — Bible 4U! Instant Drama

LARGE GROUP ■ Listen as King Hezekiah meets with three of his closest advisors.

❏ 5 actors   ❏ copies of pp. 60-61, What's the Plan? script   ❏ "Applause" and "Boo, Hiss!" posters   ❏ 4 numbered balls   Optional: ❏ Bibletime costumes, royal robes for the king   ❏ low table and cushions   ❏ scroll

2 — Shepherd's Spot

SMALL GROUP ■ Use the "A Strong Tower" handout to assure kids they can run to God for safety.

❏ Bibles   ❏ pencils   ❏ scissors   ❏ copies of p. 64, A Strong Tower   ❏ copies of p. 66, Special Delivery

Option — Workshop Wonders

SMALL GROUP ■ Play a relay game and build a tower of strength.

❏ large marshmallows   ❏ toothpicks   ❏ masking tape   ❏ table or desk   ❏ egg timer   Optional ❏ mini-marshmallows

Bible Basis
Hezekiah.
2 Kings 18:1, 3, 5;
19:10, 11, 14–16, 19,
32–35

Learn It!
God is stronger
than any nation.

Live It!
Call to God
for help.

Bible Verse
The name of the LORD is a strong tower; the righteous run to it and are safe.
Proverbs 18:10

Quick Takes

2 Kings 18:1, 3, 5; 19:10, 11, 14–16, 19, 32–35

18:1 In the third year of Hoshea son of Elah king of Israel, Hezekiah son of Ahaz king of Judah began to reign. 3 He did what was right in the eyes of the LORD, just as his father David had done. 5 Hezekiah trusted in the LORD, the God of Israel. There was no one like him among all the kings of Judah, either before him or after him. 19:10 "Say to Hezekiah king of Judah: Do not let the god you depend on deceive you when he says, 'Jerusalem will not be handed over to the king of Assyria.' 11 Surely you have heard what the kings of Assyria have done to all the countries, destroying them completely. And will you be delivered?" 14 Hezekiah received the letter from the messengers and read it. Then he went up to the temple of the LORD and spread it out before the LORD. 15 And Hezekiah prayed to the LORD: "O LORD, God of Israel, enthroned between the cherubim, you alone are God over all the kingdoms of the earth. You have made heaven and earth. 16 Give ear, O LORD, and hear; open your eyes, O LORD, and see; listen to the words Sennacherib has sent to insult the living God. 19 Now, O LORD our God, deliver us from his hand, so that all kingdoms on earth may know that you alone, O LORD, are God." 32 Therefore this is what the LORD says concerning the king of Assyria: "He will not enter this city or shoot an arrow here. He will not come before it with shield or build a siege ramp against it. 33 By the way that he came he will return; he will not enter this city, declares the LORD. 34 I will defend this city and save it, for my sake and for the sake of David my servant." 35 That night the angel of the LORD went out and put to death a hundred and eighty-five thousand men in the Assyrian camp. When the people got up the next morning—there were all the dead bodies!

Insights

The doom that the people of Jerusalem had been anticipating for years was finally upon them. The great armies of Assyria stood assembled outside the city walls. Messengers from their commanders mocked God, saying he could not save the people from the might of Assyria's army.

King Hezekiah, a man in his late twenties, took the offensive message straight to the temple of God. He poured out his prayer and received assurance of God's mercy. The battle never happened. With morning came the stunning news that the army of 185,000 Assyrians was dead.

The king's plea saved his people from destruction—at least for the time being. God kept Jerusalem safe for the duration of Hezekiah's life. Can one person's prayer make a difference? You bet! Use this lesson to encourage your kids to call on God.

There is no situation too desperate or hopeless for God's intervention.

Open with praise songs, then greet the kids. **As we'll hear in today's Bible story, God is stronger than any nation. Go to God for help when you don't know what to do and you need a safe place from trouble. Schooner, come on down!** *Schooner pops up.*

Schooner: Psst! Want to know a secret?

Leader: No.

Schooner: Come on. It's fun. I promise.

Leader: If it's a secret, Schooner, shouldn't you keep it under your hat?

Schooner: I'm not wearing a hat.

Leader: What I mean to say is a secret needs to be kept confidential.

Schooner: Big word, boss.

Leader: Private.

Schooner: Oh, this isn't that kind of secret.

Leader: No?

Schooner: No. This is something I just make up as I go along!

Leader: So, in other words, it's a tall tale.

Schooner: *(shakes tail feathers)*

Leader: You could have saved us a lot of time by just saying, "I have something to share."

Schooner: What fun is there in that? *Squawk!*

Leader: *(shakes head)* Help!

Schooner: You taught me that we should always go to God for help.

Leader: I'm glad to hear you're listening, Schooner.

Schooner: You're welcome. There's no one like me!

Leader: Or King Hezekiah.

Schooner: Huh?

Leader: In today's Bible story we read that King Hezekiah trusted in God. There was no one like him among all the kings in the land of Judah.

Schooner: A one-of-a-kind king!

Leader: And when King Hezekiah needed help to save Jerusalem, God proved more powerful than a conquering nation.

Schooner: That king had a pretty big faith.

Leader: As you wisely said before, we are to go to God for help. And he did.

Schooner: Old Testament. New Testament. Yesterday. Today. Tomorrow. Go to God for help.

Leader: Good point, Schooner. Our strong God is here for us too.

Schooner: Thanks, boss. Now, do you want to know my secret?

Leader: Are we back to that?

Schooner: Yup.

Leader: Are you sure it's not a real secret?

Schooner: Nah.

Leader: You'll tell me whether I say yes or no...

Schooner: *(shakes tail feathers in anticipation)*

Leader: Okay, Schooner.

Schooner: I'll have to sing it.

Leader: A secret song. This should be very interesting!

Schooner: I'll sing the first line and you and the group sing the second.

Leader: Will we know it?

Schooner: When you hear it!

Schooner: *(clears throat and sings to the tune of Old MacDonald)* Hezekiah was a king...

Leader and kids: E-I-E-I-O.

Schooner: A King who kept his kingdom safe.

Leader and kids: E-I-E-I-O.

Schooner: *(does a little parrot jig)* With a great God here. And a great God there. Here our God. There our God. Everywhere our God, God! Hezekiah was a king...

Leader and kids: E-I-E-I-O.

Leader: Well, Schooner, I think you kept your secret just long enough to introduce our Bible story.

Schooner: *Squawk!* Bible 4U! up next.

Permission to photocopy this script granted for local church use. Copyright © Cook Communications Ministries.
Printed in Pick Up 'n' Do Lessons on Survivor Bible Style!

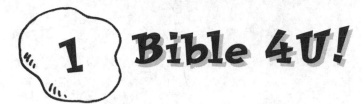

Bible 4U!

Listen carefully—the situation is desperate and we need your help in this presentation of Bible 4U! Hezekiah, king of Judah, must figure out a way to save Jerusalem and all of Judah from being taken over by the king of Assyria. The armies of Assyria have wiped out countries far and wide, and now they're massed outside the city wall of Jerusalem—all 185,000 of them! Things don't look good.

King Hezekiah is a good king and trusts in the Lord. He's destroyed all the idols in the country and led the people back to worshiping God. He's just received a message from the Assyrian commander telling him that God can't save the city from Assyria's armies. So King Hezekiah is meeting with three of his closest advisors and friends. They are each giving recommendations to him.

We need you to help decide which suggestions are good and which are bad. Watch the cards and cheer and clap for the good suggestions and boo and hiss for the bad ones. Now let's go right ahead and invite ourselves to this meeting!

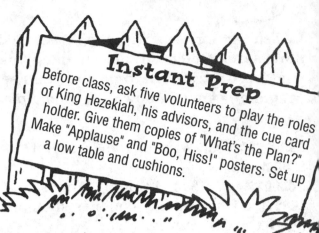

Instant Prep

Before class, ask five volunteers to play the roles of King Hezekiah, his advisors, and the cue card holder. Give them copies of "What's the Plan?" Make "Applause" and "Boo, Hiss!" posters. Set up a low table and cushions.

for Overachievers

Have a five-person drama team prepare the story. Prepare a palace set with a low table set with refreshments surrounded by floor cushions. Put a robe on King Hezekiah and make a crown for his head. Dress the others in ordinary Bibletime costumes

---

What's the Plan?
Based on 2 Kings 18:1, 3, 5; 19:10, 11, 14–16, 19, 32–35

Four men, with serious looks on their faces, are seated around a table.

King Hezekiah: We have an urgent matter before us. So I've called you, my most trusted advisors, together.

Advisors bring hands to chest and bow.

Advisors #1, 2, 3: It is our honor, O King.

Advisor #1: If we may, O King, let us review the situation. You received a message from the enemy, is that correct?

King Hezekiah: I did. A message that

insults our God. *(picks up scroll and reads)* "Don't let that god you depend on deceive you by saying, 'Jerusalem will never fall to the king of Assyria.' That's a lie. Surely you have heard what the kings of Assyria have done to all the countries, destroying them completely. What makes you think you'll be an exception?" *(puts the scroll down and begins to pray)*

Advisors discuss; King Hezekiah prays.

Advisor #2: Oooh! That's bad! We're doomed! Our lives are over. We're all going to die. *(puts head on table and begins to wail loudly)*

Advisor #3: Oh, pull yourself together, man. Our king is faithful to God! We need to call to God for help and trust in him.

Advisor #1: What we need is a plan of attack—a strategy. How big is our army?

Advisor #2: *(in a whiny voice)* Not nearly big enough. They'll kill us all for sure. I don't wanna die.

Advisor #1: We'll get everyone in the city to fight.

Card Holder walks across with the "Boo, Hiss!" poster.

Advisor #3: I think we should call on God. He will help us.

Advisor #1: *(ignoring Advisor #3)* We need to come up with more people. How can we do that? *(Pauses to think, then snaps fingers.)* I've got it! We make life-size soldiers of cardboard and line them up around the city. Our enemies will see all the soldiers from a distance and run away because we have a huge army.

Card Holder walks across with the "Boo, Hiss!" poster.

Advisor #2: We don't have enough cardboard to do that. And we certainly don't have enough time. What are we going to do?

Advisor #3: Like I said. We should call on God to help us. He's the only one who can save us.

Advisor #1: *(still ignoring Advisor #3)* You're right. We don't have a lot of time.

Advisor #2: Or weapons.

Advisor #1: We can't give up without a fight. Get the men working on weapons.

Card Holder walks across with the "Boo, Hiss!" poster.

King Hezekiah: Listen, all of you. When I received this message, I went straight to the temple and prayed to the Lord. I said: "God, You are the one and only God, sovereign over all kingdoms on earth, maker of heaven and earth. Open your ears, O Lord, and listen. Open your eyes, O Lord, and see. Look at this letter that Sennacherib has sent. It is an insult to the living God. It is true, O Lord, that the Assyrian kings have laid waste countries and kingdoms. They have thrown their gods into the fire for they were gods handmade from wood and stone. But now, O Lord our God, save us from the Assyrian power so that all the kingdoms on earth may know that you and you alone are God."

Advisor #2: That's one powerful prayer.

Advisor #1: Maybe we should pray too.

Advisor #3: Is anyone listening to me? I already suggested praying to God for help.

Card Holder walks across with the "Applause" poster.

King Hezekiah: And this is how the Lord responded. "The king of Assyria will not enter this city nor shoot a single arrow here. He'll go home by the same road that he came. I will defend this city and save it, for my sake and for David's sake."

Advisor #2: Well then, that's it. God will save the city. What a relief!

Advisor #1: Then we'll wait on God and pray. That's our best strategic plan.

Advisor #3: God is stronger than any nation.

Card Holder walks across with the "Applause!" poster. All four exit. After a brief pause, Advisor #3 walks back onstage.

Advisor #3: Last night the angel of the Lord went through the Assyrian camp. When we woke this morning, all the Assyrian soldiers were dead. Praise to Jehovah God who saved us by his power and gave us a king who is firm in his faith. *(bows slightly and exits)*

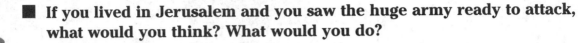

You guys were a great help. Thanks for your participation. Now I'm sure you have a good grasp of King Hezekiah's strategic plan.

Toss the four numbered balls to different parts of the room. Bring kids with the balls to the front one-by-one and ask these questions. Allow kids to get help from the group if they need it. After each correct answer, let kids drop their balls into a bag.

■ If you lived in Jerusalem and you saw the huge army ready to attack, what would you think? What would you do?

■ What do you think of King Hezekiah as a leader? Explain.

■ What do you think the people said when they discovered that the angel of the Lord had wiped out the Assyrian army?

■ Tell about a time when you called to God for help. How did he answer your call?

King Hezekiah's faith made a huge difference in this story. Listen to what the Bible says about him. "Hezekiah trusted in the LORD, the god of Israel. There was no one like him among all the kings of Judah, either before him or after him. He held fast to the Lord and did not cease to follow him. He kept the commands the Lord had given Moses. And the Lord was with him" (2 Kings 18:5-7). That's the kind of person I'd like to have for a leader!

The whole country was depending on King Hezekiah. And they survived because of God's faithfulness. Can you even begin to imagine how the people of Jerusalem felt when they woke the next morning and found that the angel of the Lord had wiped out the enemy? They learned that God is more powerful than the mightiest nation.

Bible Verse
The name of the LORD is a strong tower; the righteous run to it and are safe.
Proverbs 18:10

Today in your shepherd groups you'll make a cool castle to remind you that God is like a strong tower; we can go to him for safety.

Dismiss kids to their shepherd groups.

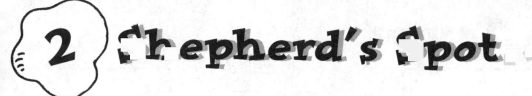

Gather your small group and help kids find 2 Kings 18 in their Bibles.

Hezekiah was a very cool king. And there were a lot of bad kings, you know—kings who led the people away from God. When disaster was ready to strike, King Hezekiah knew right where to turn—to almighty God.

Have volunteers take turns reading 2 Kings 18:1, 3, 5; 19:10, 11, 14–16, 19, 32–35.

■ **If you were in Jerusalem surrounded by an army, would you feel safer with a big army of your own or with praying and trusting God. Be honest!**

King Hezekiah knew something that lots of people have trouble understanding: God is more powerful than any power on earth. He knew he could turn to God in a desperate situation. Guess what—you can too!

Distribute the "A Strong Tower" handouts. Have a volunteer read the verse on the drawbridge aloud. *"The name of the LORD is a strong tower. The righteous run to it and are safe"* (Proverbs 18:10).

Lead kids through the following steps to assemble their towers.

1. Cut out background, the drawbridge and the castle gate. Fold the background in.

2. Fold the drawbridge in half so the verse shows. Fold the end tabs forward and glue them to the drawbridge space on the background.

3. Fold back the tabs on the castle gate. Glue them to the spaces marked on the background.

4. Have kids draw their last names on the pennant in the foreground.

■ **When do you need to run to God for safety?**

Today let's pray for people who need God's protection. When I pause, you fill in names, either silently or out loud. Heavenly father, it's so wonderful to know that you are a strong tower and that we can run to you for safety. Give us faith like King Hezekiah had. And watch over people who need your protection. We're thinking of (pause for kids to mention their concerns). We praise you and we put our trust in you. In Jesus' name, amen.

Permission to photocopy this lesson page granted for local church use. Copyright © Cook Communications Ministries.
Printed in Pick Up 'n' Do Lessons on Survivor Bible Style!

A Strong Tower

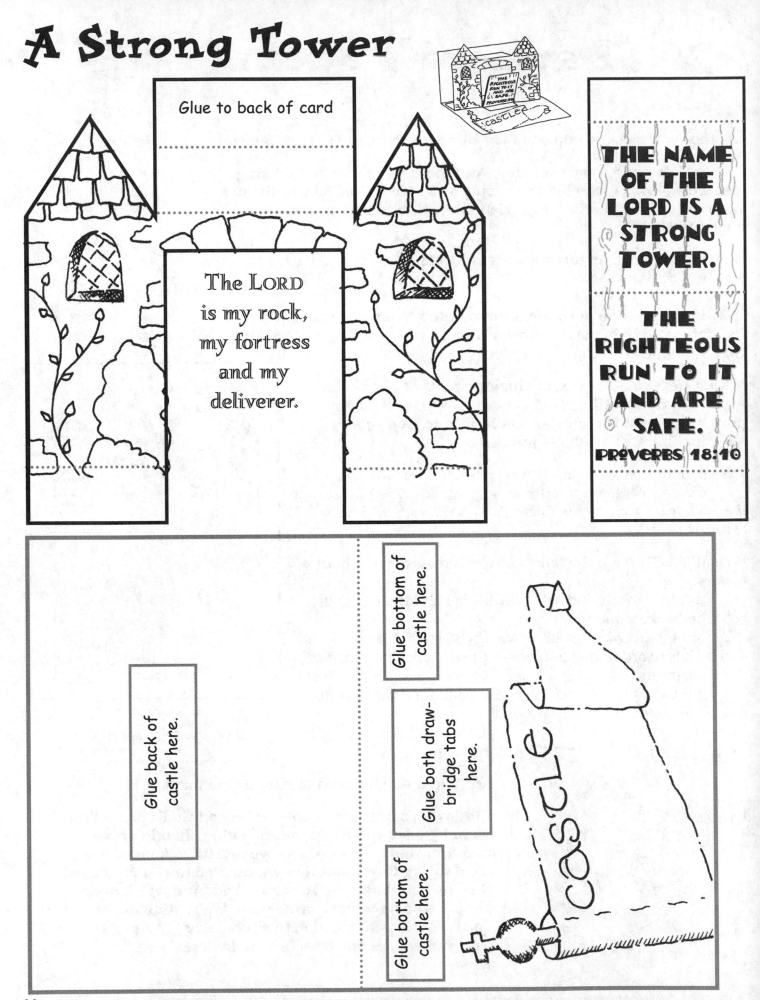

Glue to back of card

The LORD is my rock, my fortress and my deliverer.

THE NAME OF THE LORD IS A STRONG TOWER.

THE RIGHTEOUS RUN TO IT AND ARE SAFE.
PROVERBS 18:10

Glue back of castle here.

Glue bottom of castle here.

Glue bottom of castle here.

Glue both draw- bridge tabs here.

castle

Adapted from Paper Capers © Lois Keffer Printed by Cook Communications Ministries. Used by permission. Permission to photocopy this handout granted for local church use. Copyright © Cook Communications Ministries. Printed in Pick Up 'n' Do Lessons on Survivor Bible Style!

An advancing army surrounds Jerusalem. What's a king to do—lose his mind? There's no authority higher in all the land. Where does a king go for help? King Hezekiah knew.

■ **How would your city or town respond if an enemy army was headed its way?**

Get List:
- ❑ bags of large marshmallows
- ❑ boxes of toothpicks
- ❑ masking tape
- ❑ table
- ❑ egg timer
- Optional
- ❑ mini-marshmallows

As King Hezekiah ruled over Judah, he turned to God when he needed divine help. He had seen first-hand what God could do. Like a strong tower, God could be counted on to help shelter and protect him and his people.

Review today's Bible verse with your class: *"The name of the LORD is a strong tower; the righteous run to it and are safe"* (Proverbs 18:10).

Mark off a starting line on one side of the room. Place a table or desk on the opposite end. Then separate your class into two or three relay teams. You'll need a bag of marshmallows and toothpicks for each team. Place them on the table. Teams will use the marshmallows and toothpicks to build a tower, which they will run to—as today's Bible Verse describes!

Team members, your job is to keep at it! Run to the table and add more marshmallows and toothpicks. See how high your tower goes. Be sure to encourage your team. By the time you hear the timer ring, everyone should have had a chance to add to the tower. On your mark, get set...go!

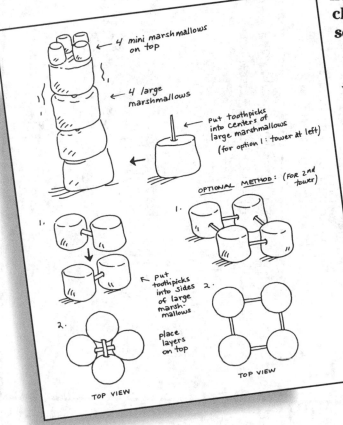

4 mini marshmallows on top

4 large marshmallows

Put toothpicks into centers of large marshmallows (for option I: tower at left)

OPTIONAL METHOD: (for 2nd tower)

1.

put toothpicks into sides of large marsh-mallows

2.

place layers on top

TOP VIEW

TOP VIEW

Determine a time and let your kids play. Let them vote on the various categories such as the strongest tower, the one that leans the most, the most unique shape, and the one that looks most likely to collapse. **Remember what you need to do when you need help. Run to God! He is our strong tower.**

Helpful Hint: For higher towers, open the marshmallow bag the night before class. Stale marshmallows work well for this activity—the firmer, harder marshmallows stack much better than fresh ones.

Permission to photocopy this lesson page granted for local church use. Copyright © Cook Communications Ministries.
Printed in Pick Up 'n' Do Lessons on Survivor Bible Style!

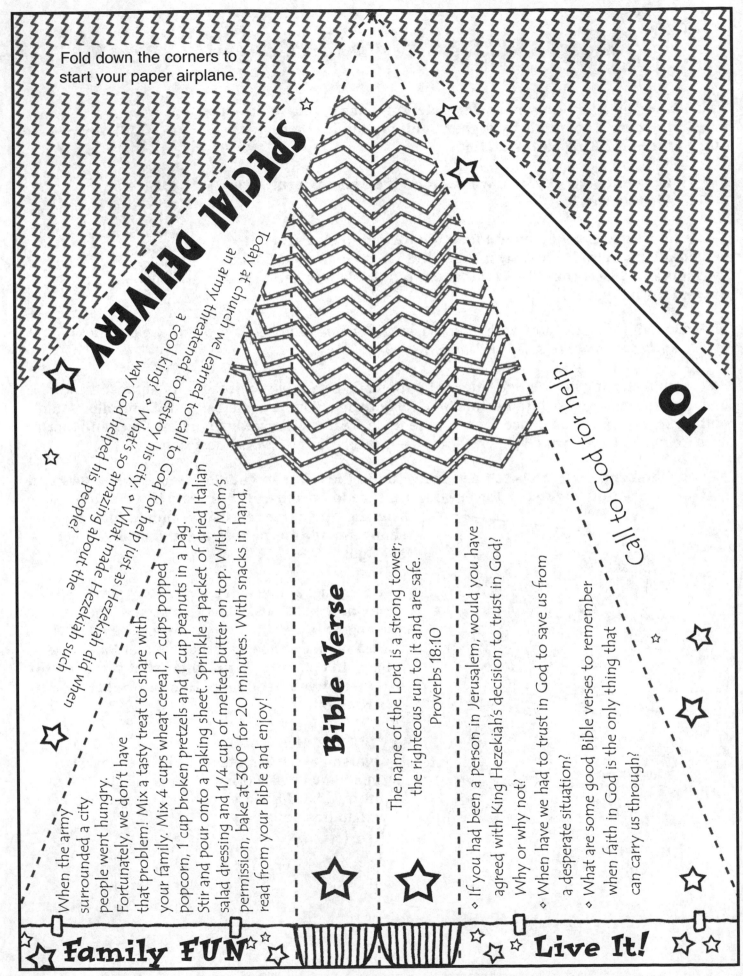

Fold down the corners to start your paper airplane.

SPECIAL DELIVERY

TO

Call to God for help.

Bible Verse

The name of the Lord is a strong tower; the righteous run to it and are safe.
Proverbs 18:10

◊ If you had been a person in Jerusalem, would you have agreed with King Hezekiah's decision to trust in God? Why or why not?

◊ When have we had to trust in God to save us from a desperate situation?

◊ What are some good Bible verses to remember when faith in God is the only thing that can carry us through?

Today at church we learned to call to God for help just as Hezekiah did when an army threatened to destroy his city. ◇ What's so amazing about the way God helped his people? ◇ What made Hezekiah such a cool king?

When the army surrounded a city people went hungry. Fortunately, we don't have that problem! Mix a tasty treat to share with your family. Mix 4 cups wheat cereal, 2 cups popped popcorn, 1 cup broken pretzels and 1 cup peanuts in a bag. Stir and pour onto a baking sheet. Sprinkle a packet of dried Italian salad dressing and 1/4 cup of melted butter on top. With Mom's permission, bake at 300° for 20 minutes. With snacks in hand, read from your Bible and enjoy!

Family FUN

Live It!

Permission to photocopy this handout granted for local church use. Copyright © Cook Communications Ministries.
Printed in Pick Up 'n' Do Lessons on Survivor Bible Style!

Treasure in the Temple

Get Set
LARGE GROUP ■ Greet kids and do a puppet skit. Birdcalls help Schooner see that God calls us to love him.

❑ large bird puppet   ❑ puppeteer

Bible 4U! Instant Drama
LARGE GROUP ■ A talking scroll tells the story of the repairs made to the temple by King Josiah.

❑ 4 actors   ❑ copies of pp. 70-71, The Scroll Unrolled script   ❑ 4 numbered balls
Optional: ❑ large sheet of newsprint or white blanket   ❑ 2 Bibletime costumes
❑ royal robes and crown   ❑ backdrop with a pillar that suggests the temple
❑ cloth or paper towel

Shepherd's Spot
SMALL GROUP ■ Use the "A Heart for God" handout to help kids learn that God expects us to love him with all our hearts.

❑ Bibles   ❑ pencils   ❑ scissors   ❑ copies of p. 74, Heart for God   ❑ copies of p. 76, Special Delivery

Workshop Wonders
SMALL GROUP ■ A yummy reconstruction of the temple culminates in a praise celebration.

❑ Bibles   ❑ graham crackers   ❑ marshmallow creme   ❑ aluminum foil   ❑ large pretzel sticks   ❑ gum drops   ❑ gummi bear candies

Bible Basis
Josiah repairs the temple. 2 Kings 22:1–15, 19, 23:1–3, 25

Learn It!
God calls us to love him.

Live It!
Turn to the Lord with all your heart.

Bible Verse
What does the LORD your God ask of you but to fear the LORD your God, to walk in all his ways, to love him, to serve the LORD your God with all your heart and with all your soul?
Deuteronomy 10:12

Quick Takes

2 Kings 22:1–15, 19, 23:1–3, 25

Josiah was eight years old when he became king...He did what was right in the eyes of the LORD and walked in all the ways of his father David... In the eighteenth year of his reign, King Josiah sent the secretary, Shaphan...to the temple of the LORD He said: "Go up to Hilkiah the high priest and make him get ready the money that has been brought into the temple of the LORD, which the doorkeepers have collected from the people. Make them entrust it to the men appointed to supervise the work on the temple. And make these men pay the workers who repair the temple of the LORD—the carpenters, the builders and the masons. Also make them purchase timber and dressed stone to repair the temple"...Hilkiah the high priest said to Shaphan the secretary, "I have found the Book of the Law in the temple of the LORD." He gave it to Shaphan, who read it. (22:1-6)

Then Shaphan the secretary informed the king, "Hilkiah the priest has given me a book." And Shaphan read from it in the presence of the king. When the king heard the words of the Book of the Law, he tore his robes. He gave these orders..."Go and inquire of the LORD for me and for the people and for all Judah about what is written in this book that has been found. Great is the LORD's anger that burns against us because our fathers have not obeyed the words of this book..." Hilkiah the priest, Ahikam, Acbor, Shaphan and Asaiah went to speak to the prophetess Huldah (22:10-14)

She said to them, "This is what the LORD, the God of Israel, says: Tell the man who sent you to me, Because your heart was responsive and you humbled yourself before the LORD when you heard what I have spoken against this place and its people, that they would become accursed and laid waste, and because you tore your robes and wept in my presence, I have heard you." (22:15, 19)

Then the king called together all the elders of Judah and Jerusalem. He went up to the temple of the LORD with the men of Judah, the people of Jerusalem, the priests and the prophets—all the people from the least to the greatest. He read in their hearing all the words of the Book of the Covenant, which had been found in the temple of the LORD. The king stood by the pillar and renewed the covenant in the presence of the LORD—to follow the LORD and keep his commands, regulations and decrees with all his heart and all his soul...Then all the people pledged themselves to the covenant. Neither before nor after Josiah was there a king like him who turned to the LORD as he did—with all his heart and with all his soul and with all his strength. (23:1-3, 25)

Insights

After a string of unfaithful kings who led Judah deeply into idol worship, an eight-year-old boy came to the throne. In his 31-year reign, Josiah restored temple worship, renewed the covenant between God and his people and banished idols from the land.

During the reigns of previous kings, the temple had been desecrated with idols and had fallen into disrepair from years of neglect. In his twenties, Josiah set about righting that situation. As workers cleaned and repaired, a precious treasure came to light: a scroll of the Law, probably the book of Deuteronomy. As his secretary read from the scroll, Josiah tore his clothes in dismay. God's people had wandered so far from the Law that Josiah didn't see how God would let them survive.

Josiah moved into action, reading the law in front of the people, renewing the covenant by a pillar of the temple, and celebrating a joyous Passover. One man who loved God with all his heart turned the hearts of a nation, and God blessed them.

God calls to kids today just as he gently called an eight-year-old king. Use this lesson to urge kids to respond to God by determining to love and follow him with all their hearts.

Option Get Set •••••••••••

Open with lively music, then greet your kids sounding like a parrot. *Squawk!* **Hello, Christy! Hello, Caleb! It's Parrot Time! God calls us to love him. Turn to God with all your heart. Squawk!** (Normal voice) **Schooner, I have a bird question for you today.** *Schooner pops up.*

Schooner: Nice try, boss.

Leader: I've been practicing! Now for my question. A friend asked me the other day…

Schooner: Yes?

Leader: …if you do birdcalls.

Schooner: What do I look like, a goat?

Leader: I know you can squawk, but birdcalls.

Schooner: Well I took three years of meadowlark in grade school and I studied a year abroad.

Leader: And what did you learn there?

Schooner: The hula and the mother tongue of the Australian cockatiel.

Leader: Can you do some for us now?

Schooner: The hula?

Leader: No.

Schooner: What then?

Leader: The voice of the Australian cockatiel.

Schooner: Right now?

Leader: Yes.

Schooner: Here?

Leader: Schooner!?

Schooner: Okay. Don't get your feathers in a bunch. *(takes a breath)* Cockle-doodle-do! Cockle-doodle-dooooo!

Leader: *(scratches head)* I think you have your calls mixed up, Schooner.

Schooner: Hmm?

Leader: That's a rooster's call.

Schooner: Not in Australia!

Leader: Well, it sounds very close.

Schooner: Blame it on the rooster.

Leader: *(shakes head)*

Schooner: Parrot got your tongue, boss?

Leader: I think I'm safe if I stick with today's Bible story. God calls us to love him.

Schooner: Hmm. What would that call sound like, boss?

Leader: Well in today's story the first call comes from workers inside a rundown old temple.

Schooner: Tell me again, what's a temple?

Leader: A temple is a place of worship. But that hadn't happened in our story in quite a while.

Schooner: Oh.

Leader: Now the good part. Something incredible was found in the rubble.

Schooner: A treasure?

Leader: Something that had been missing for many years. The book of God's Law.

Schooner: Was it covered in gold and precious gems?

Leader: The Bible doesn't say that the book's cover was valuable.

Schooner: Then where's the treasure?

Leader: The treasure was between the covers.

Schooner: You mean the words.

Leader: Yes. God's law was a covenant, an agreement between him and his people. It was a holy promise on how his people should live and love him.

Schooner: Words from God. Wow! That is a find!

Leader: And Josiah, that's today's Bible character, was determined to dust the book off and put its words into action.

Schooner: You know what, boss?

Leader: Yes?

Schooner: Our Bible stories keep getting better and better.

Leader: God's words are for all time. They teach us to live in his love.

Schooner: *(turns mouth to the side)* Briing! Briing! The call's for you, boss!

Leader: *(pretends to pick up the phone)* Hello. What's that? Bible 4U! up next?

Schooner: *Squawk!* Works like a charm everytime!

Permission to photocopy this script granted for local church use. Copyright © Cook Communications Ministries. Printed in Pick Up 'n' Do Lessons on Survivor Bible Style!

1 Bible 4U!

Welcome to another exciting episode of Bible 4U! Today's story takes us into a dusty, crumbling building that's falling apart from years of not being cared for. Sadly, the building I'm talking about was God's temple in Jerusalem. When King Solomon built the temple, it had shining columns, gleaming gold, and carved woodwork made by the finest craftsmen. But over the years kings who didn't follow God ignored the temple, or even worse, set up idols and worshiped them right there in God's house.

Instant Prep

Before class, ask four volunteers to play the roles of the Scroll, Hilkiah, Shaphan and King Josiah. Give them copies of the script below. Wrap the Scroll actor hot-dog style in a sheet of newsprint.

for Overachievers

Have a four-person drama team prepare the story. Wrap the Scroll actor in an off-white blanket. Dress Josiah in kingly robes. Give Shaphan and Hilkiah Bibletime costumes. Create backdrop with a pillar that suggests the temple.

As the years slipped by, people forgot how to worship God. They didn't know his laws. They didn't know how to make sacrifices or celebrate feasts to thank God for his care. Finally an eight-year-old boy became king. King Josiah loved God. When he grew to manhood, he gave orders for the temple to be repaired.

King Josiah had no idea that his orders would lead to the discovery of a great treasure that would change his whole kingdom...

The Scroll Unrolled
Based on 2 Kings 22:1–15, 19, 23:1–3, 25

Scroll enters shuffling inside the blanket.

Scroll: Do you have any idea what it feels like to be crunched in a corner for so many years you've lost count? Here I am, rolled up, smashed by crumbling walls, and nibbled on by mice. What really makes me sad is that God's people have forgotten all about me. My pages contain the Law of God written down by Moses. The Law tells how God's people are special to him, how they are to serve and worship him and keep his festivals. People today don't remember any of that stuff. They're so far from God that they can hardly call themselves his people anymore. So here I wait in my dusty corner of the temple, hoping that someday someone will find me and the treasure I contain.

Nobody even comes in here to clean anymore. I remember when this temple was the most beautiful building in Israel. When the people forgot God, they forgot this place, too. Some evil kings even set up idols here—in the very house of God. I just hope that someday—SOMEDAY—someone will find me.

Uh-oh. Here comes a piece of a wall. DUCK! Is that the sound of a broom I hear?

Whoa—some stuff is being pulled off me. They're pulling me out of here. I'm in someone's hands!

Hilkiah: What have we here?
Shaphan: Pull a little harder.
Scroll: Ouch!
Hilkiah: Wow—this thing is filthy.
Scroll: *(to audience)* He'd be dusty too if he'd been standing in a corner for as many years as I have.
Shaphan: Let's wipe it down. Then we can open it and see just exactly what we've found.

They rub scroll with a cloth.

Scroll: *(to audience)* Ooh—that feels so good! A little higher on the left there...
Hilkiah: Ready to open it.
Scroll: Ho boy, this is gonna be a stretch. I haven't unwrapped myself in...oooh! Ah! Easy there, boys.

They unwrap the blanket on the floor. Scroll stretches and sighs.

Shaphan: This is ancient writing. Beautiful! But...oh my goodness!
Hilkiah: It's the Law of God!
Shaphan: The writings of Moses.
Hilkiah: I wonder how many years this has been lost?
Shaphan: We have to tell the king!

They exit. Scroll stands and speaks.

Scroll: The priest and the king's secretary took me to the palace. Shaphan read my words aloud to the king. He was so upset that he tore his robes and cried. Why? Because he realized how much his country had sinned. Then God sent the king a message that said, "Because your heart was broken and you cried and humbled yourself before me, I have heard you. I will give your country peace during your lifetime."

The king, Hilkiah and Shaphan enter as Scroll steps back.

King: Because the people of our country have been unfaithful to God, we all deserve to die. But God is loving and full of mercy. He has promised that we will not be destroyed. Now there is much to be done! Get all the idols out of the temple. Destroy all the hilltop shrines. Smash and burn anything that has to do with pagan gods. We must purify our land.
Hilkiah: It shall be done, my Lord.
King: We will call all the people together at the temple and renew our covenant with God.
Shaphan: I will send word to every priest and elder in the land.

They freeze. Scroll steps forward.

Scroll: Everything was done just as the king ordered. All the elders and priests came together in front of the temple. The king stood by a pillar and read all the words of the Law from my pages. He and all the people promised to follow God and to be God's people. It was a great day in Jerusalem.

King: *(steps forward and reads to the audience)* And now, O Israel, what does the LORD your God ask of you but to fear the LORD your God, to walk in all his ways, to love him, to serve the LORD your God with all your heart and with all your soul? (Deut. 10:12)

Scroll: And that's just what they did. While King Josiah ruled, the people joyfully followed God. They held a great feast to remember how God took his people out of slavery in Egypt. And me? People read my pages all the time! You have a book a lot like me at your house, maybe even with you today—a book that contains the Word of God. Don't leave me on a shelf or in a dusty corner! Read me and learn how much God loves you and wants you to serve him with all your heart.

Hilkiah and Shaphan wrap the Scroll in the blanket and they all exit.

Permission to photocopy this script granted for local church use. Copyright © Cook Communications Ministries.
Printed in Pick Up 'n' Do Lessons on Survivor Bible Style!

That was quite a discovery. Workmen found the old scroll that contained the precious Word of God. No one even knew how many years it had been lost. Let's see what discoveries you made today.

Toss the four numbered balls to different parts of the room. Bring the kids with the balls to the front one by one and ask these questions. Allow kids to get help from the group if they need it. After each correct answer, let kids drop their balls into a bag.

■ **How did the scroll get lost?**

■ **Why was King Josiah upset when he heard God's law?**

■ **How did the king show that he wanted to follow God with all his heart?**

■ **What does it mean to you to follow God with all your heart?**

All of us have times we might call "oops" moments. Like if you kick the ball into the wrong goal, or forget your mom's birthday or blurt out something that hurts a friend's feelings. Hearing the Law for the first time was a gigantic "oops" moment for King Josiah. His people had really messed up! The Law said to love God more than anything else. It told about special feasts when the people could thank God for his goodness. It told about how to treat others. It even said what to eat and what not to eat! God gave the Law to his people so they could be an example to other nations. But when the Law was ignored and forgotten, the Israelites worshiped idols and did the same terrible things as all the other nations.

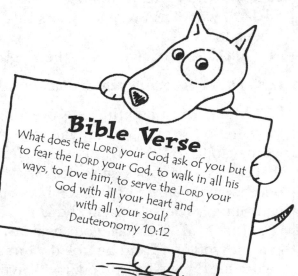

Bible Verse
What does the LORD your God ask of you but to fear the LORD your God, to walk in all his ways, to love him, to serve the LORD your God with all your heart and with all your soul?
Deuteronomy 10:12

God waited patiently until a little boy became king—a little boy who truly loved God and wanted to serve him. When the king realized how badly his people had sinned, he started immediately to set things right. He put his whole heart into turning the nation back towards God, teaching them the Law and what it meant to be God's special people. The king's determination to follow God with all his heart made a huge difference. God blessed the people and kept them in his care.

Dismiss kids to their shepherd groups.

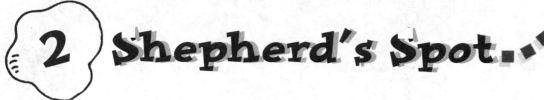

2 Shepherd's Spot

Gather your small group and help kids find 2 Kings 22 in their Bibles.

In the books of First and Second kings we learn all about—you guessed it—the kings who ruled God's people. We see that the choices the king made affected all the people of the country. Bad kings led the people into idol worship, far away from God. Good kings turned the nation's heart toward God. King Josiah was one of the best kings ever. Let's read his story straight from God's Word.

Have volunteers take turns reading 2 Kings 22:1–6, 15, 19; 23:1–3, 25 aloud.

■ **Suppose you had stood in front of the temple and listened to King Josiah read the Law. What would you have told your family when you went home?**

■ **Worshiping idols kept God's people from following him with all their hearts. What keeps people from following God with all their hearts today?**

Pass out the "Heart for God" handout. Have kids cut it out and assemble it according to the directions on the handout. **Wow—this heart pops right out! And it tells us what's really important.** Ask a volunteer to read Deuteronomy 10:12 aloud: *"What does the LORD your God ask of you but to fear the LORD your God, to walk in all his ways, to love him, to serve the LORD your God with all your heart and with all your soul?"*

Keep this in a special spot where it can remind you that serving God with all your heart is the most important thing you can do. One way we serve God is by praying for others. Let's do that right now.

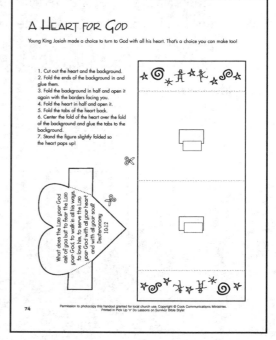

Invite kids to share prayer concerns. Then close with prayer. **Dear Lord, we're thankful for all the good things that happened when King Josiah read your Word. Help us keep your Word before us every day, because we know it has the power to turn our hearts toward you. Lord, today we pray for (mention kids' concerns). Now bless our week we pray, and help us to serve you with all our hearts. In Jesus' name, amen.**

Permission to photocopy this lesson page granted for local church use. Copyright © Cook Communications Ministries.
Printed in Pick Up 'n' Do Lessons on Survivor Bible Style!

A Heart for God

Young King Josiah made a choice to turn to God with all his heart. That's a choice you can make too!

1. Cut out the heart and the background.
2. Fold the ends of the background in and glue them.
3. Fold the background in half and open it again with the borders facing you.
4. Fold the heart in half and open it.
5. Fold the tabs of the heart back.
6. Center the fold of the heart over the fold of the background and glue the tabs to the background.
7. Stand the figure slightly folded so the heart pops up!

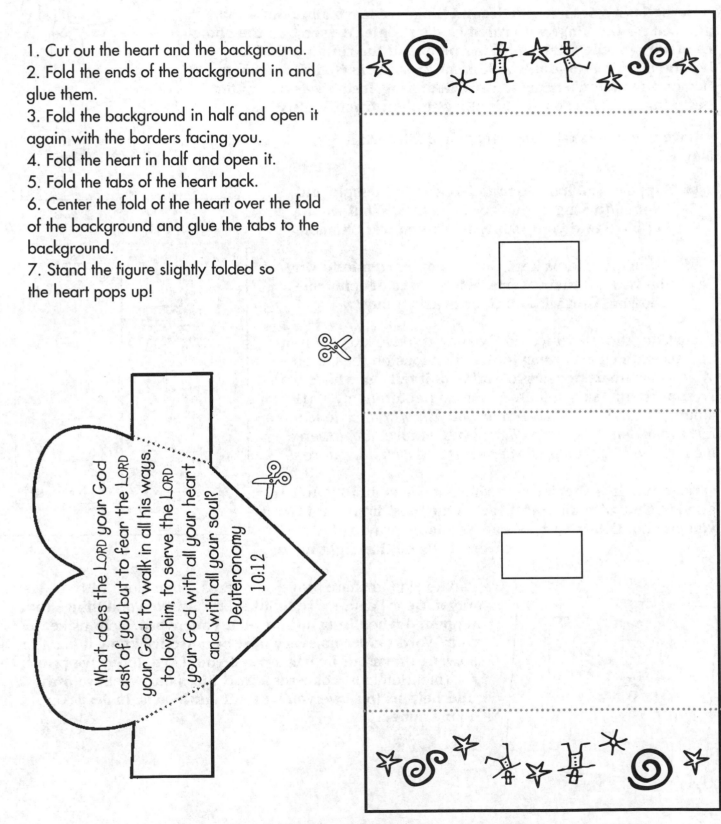

What does the LORD your God ask of you but to fear the LORD your God, to walk in all his ways, to love him, to serve the LORD your God with all your heart and with all your soul? Deuteronomy 10:12

Permission to photocopy this handout granted for local church use. Copyright © Cook Communications Ministries. Printed in Pick Up 'n' Do Lessons on Survivor Bible Style!

Workshop Wonders

The temple in Jerusalem was a holy place to God's people. They believed God was present in the temple, so they went there every day to worship and offer sacrifices. Wicked kings before Josiah had taken out the things used to worship God and filled the temple with idols instead.

Get List:
- ❑ graham crackers
- ❑ marshmallow creme
- ❑ aluminum foil
- ❑ large pretzel sticks
- ❑ gumdrops
- ❑ fresh gummi bear candies

When King Josiah took over, he felt badly about how the temple had been treated. The building was old, and it hadn't been repaired in years. Josiah set to work to change that, and in the process the workers found the scroll that contained God's laws. By the time the work was finished, the temple was clean and shining, and the people gathered to celebrate, worship and promise to follow God.

Let's have a celebration of our own by building a model of God's temple. It was a tall building with great pillars. And it was surrounded by courtyards that were separated by walls. Use your best architectural skills and start building! If you have a large group of kids, you may want to have them work in groups of five.

The finishing touch on our temple is the people who came to worship. Let's use gummi bears to represent people gathering at the temple. Pause for kids to add crowds. The king and the priests read scripture, and there was a lot of singing and praising God. Let's sing a favorite praise song and imagine we were there all those years ago rejoicing that God's house was beautiful again! Lead kids in one or two favorite songs. Add rhythm instruments and happy movement to the songs.

The temple is no longer standing in the city of Jerusalem. But that's all right. God doesn't live there any more. He lives in our hearts. And he wants us to love him and serve him with all our hearts, just as our Bible verse says.

Challenge kids to repeat Deuteronomy 10:12: "*What does the LORD your God ask of you but to fear the LORD your God, to walk in all his ways, to love him, to serve the LORD your God with all your heart and with all your soul?*"

Now let's give thanks and go ahead and devour our masterpieces!

Remember, your heart is God's temple. Go and serve him with all your heart.

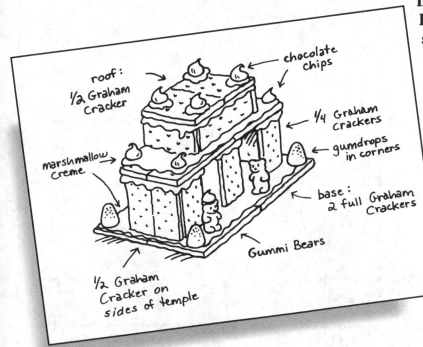

roof: 1/2 Graham Cracker
chocolate chips
1/4 Graham Crackers
gumdrops in corners
marshmallow creme
base: 2 full Graham Crackers
Gummi Bears
1/2 Graham Cracker on sides of temple

Permission to photocopy this lesson page granted for local church use. Copyright © Cook Communications Ministries.
Printed in Pick Up 'n' Do Lessons on Survivor Bible Style!

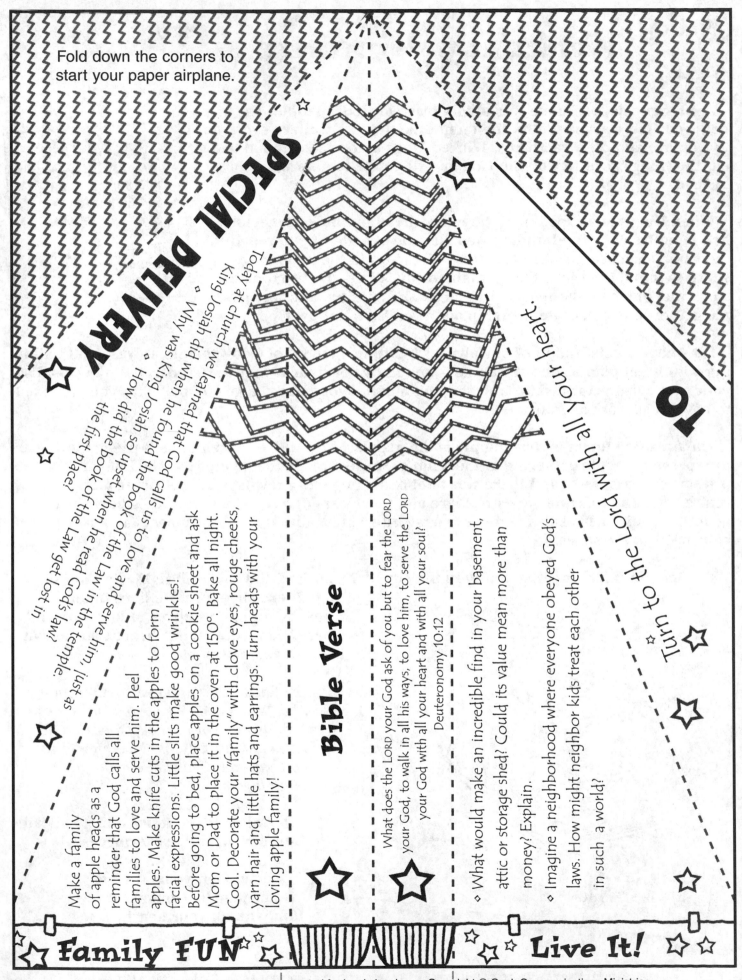

Fold down the corners to start your paper airplane.

SPECIAL DELIVERY

TO

Turn to the Lord with all your heart.

Why was King Josiah so upset when he read God's law? How did the book of the Law in the temple. King Josiah did when he found the book of the Law get lost in the first place? Today at church we learned that God calls us to love and serve him, just as

Make a family of apple heads as a reminder that God calls all families to love and serve him. Peel apples. Make knife cuts in the apples to form facial expressions. Little slits make good wrinkles! Before going to bed, place apples on a cookie sheet and ask Mom or Dad to place it in the oven at 150°. Bake all night. Cool. Decorate your "family" with clove eyes, rouge cheeks, yarn hair and little hats and earrings. Turn heads with your loving apple family!

Bible Verse

What does the Lord your God ask of you but to fear the Lord your God, to walk in all his ways, to love him, to serve the Lord your God with all your heart and with all your soul? Deuteronomy 10:12

◇ What would make an incredible find in your basement, attic or storage shed? Could its value mean more than money? Explain.

◇ Imagine a neighborhood where everyone obeyed God's laws. How might neighbor kids treat each other in such a world?

Family FUN

Live It!

Permission to photocopy this handout granted for local church use. Copyright © Cook Communications Ministries.
Printed in Pick Up 'n' Do Lessons on Survivor Bible Style!

The Queen and Mr. Mean

Get Set
LARGE GROUP ■ Greet kids and do a puppet skit. An imaginative parade helps Schooner see that good conquers evil with God's help.

❏ large bird puppet   ❏ puppeteer

Bible 4U! Instant Drama
LARGE GROUP ■ Let a cast of daring characters (a King, a Queen, a hero and a villain) share this survivor story.

❏ 3 actors   ❏ copies of pp. 80-81, Saved by the Queen script   ❏ 4 numbered balls
Optional: ❏ 2 Bibletime costumes   ❏ elegant robe or fabric for the queen
❏ costume jewelry   ❏ crown   ❏ strip of burlap   ❏ bundle of papers

Shepherd's Spot
SMALL GROUP ■ Use the "And the Queen Wins!" handout to review the Bible story with your class.

❏ Bibles   ❏ pencils   ❏ scissors   ❏ copies of p. 84, And the Queen Wins!   ❏ copies of p. 86, Special Delivery

Workshop Wonders
SMALL GROUP ■ An experiment with oil, water and salt illustrates how God uses his people as a force for good.

❏ small glass jars   ❏ vegetable oil   ❏ box of salt   ❏ pitcher of water

Bible Basis
The Book of Esther

Learn It!
God defeats evil people.

Live It!
Be a force for good.

Bible Verse
Do not be overcome by evil, but overcome evil with good. Romans 12:21

Quick Takes

Now the king set a royal crown on Ester's head and made her queen. After these events, King Xerxes honored Haman...giving him a seat of honor higher than that of all the other nobles. When Haman saw that Mordecai would not kneel down or pay him honor, he was enraged. Yet having learned who Mordecai's people were, he scorned the idea of killing only Mordecai. Instead Haman looked for a way to destroy all Mordecai's people, the Jews, throughout the whole kingdom of Xerxes. (2:17, 3:1, 5-6)

When Mordecai learned of all that had been done, he tore his clothes, put on sackcloth and ashes, and went out into the city, wailing loudly and bitterly. Then Esther summoned Hathach...and ordered him to find out what was troubling Mordecai and why. Mordecai told him everything that had happened to him...He also gave him a copy of the text of the edict for their annihilation, which had been published in Susa, to show to Esther and explain it to her, and he told him to urge her to go into the king's presence to beg for mercy and plead with him for her people. (4:1, 5, 7, 8, 15-16, 5:2)

The king and Haman went to dine with Queen Esther, and as they were drinking wine on that second day, the king again asked, "Queen Esther, what is your petition? It will be given you..." Then Queen Esther answered, "If I have found favor with you, O king, and if it pleases your majesty, grant me my life—this is my petition. And spare my people—this is my request. For I and my people have been sold for destruction and slaughter and annihilation." King Xerxes asked Queen Esther, "Who is he? Where is the man who has dared to do such a thing?" Esther said, "The adversary and enemy is this vile Haman." Then Haman was terrified before the king and queen...So they hanged Haman on the gallows he had prepared for Mordecai. (7:1-6, 10)

The king's edict granted the Jews in every city the right to assemble and protect themselves...Mordecai recorded these events, and he sent letters to all the Jews throughout the provinces of King Xerxes, near and far, to have them celebrate annually the fourteenth and fifteenth days of the month of Adar as the time when the Jews got relief from their enemies, and as the month when their sorrow was turned into joy and their mourning into a day of celebration. (8:11, 9:20-22).

Insights

Queen Esther won the king's heart after he set aside his previous queen for disobeying him. Only Esther and her cousin Mordecai knew Esther's secret identity: she was a Jew. Along comes Haman, one of those people who is so inflated with his own pride that he's bound to create his own downfall. And that's just what he did. Offended because Mordecai would not bow down to him, Haman wasn't content just to go after Mordecai. He set his sights on destroying the entire Jewish race—these people who bowed to no one but their God.

Bolstered by the prayers of her people and her maids, Esther approached the king uninvited. He received her and then accepted her invitation to dine with her and with Haman.

Thus began Esther's ingenious game of cat and mouse, which ended with an enraged king hanging Haman on his own gallows.

The king could not revoke the edict he'd already signed that allowed the destruction of the Jews. But he could and did sign a new edict declaring that the Jews could defend themselves. Rising as a nation, the Jews killed their enemies. Since that day, the Jewish people commemorate this victory with the feast of Purim.

A single child may feel powerless to face down evil. Use this story to teach them that one person backed by prayer can be a great force for good.

Get Set

Open with lively music, then greet the kids. **God is bigger than all the wrong in the world. We need to remember that when the world seems a scary place. When it comes to facing evil, you'd be surprised at what a difference one person can make. Schooner, join us.**
Schooner pops up.

Schooner: Today it's pets on parade!

Leader: *(looks around the room)* I don't see a parade, Schooner.

Schooner: It's in my head.

Leader: *(leans over and looks in Schooner's ear)* Oh, there it is!

Schooner: Smarty pants!

Leader: Tell us what you have *(pauses for emphasis)* "in mind," Schooner.

Schooner: A cat, a dog, a donkey too, a crab, a cow, a dinosaur blue! *Squawk!*

Leader: What an active imagination you have.

Schooner: You can do it too. Close your eyes.

Leader: Let's ask the group to help us.

Schooner: *(looks out to the group)* Eyes closed! Eyes closed! *Squawk!*

Leader: Eyes closed everybody.

Schooner: Now imagine your favorite animals on parade. Purple elephants, spotted giraffes, smelly skunks—it'll make you laugh!

Leader: *(pauses as group imagines silly pets on parade)*

Schooner: It's fun!

Leader: Open eyes everyone. It was fun, Schooner, but I didn't imagine pets.

Schooner: What did you think about?

Leader: A King and Queen.

Schooner: Good name for a dog parade, boss.

Leader: These are people in today's Bible story. And the story is about evil.

Schooner: Let me guess. In the end, good conquers evil.

Leader: Yes.

Schooner: And the people rejoice and celebrate!

Leader: Yes.

Schooner: Because the king saves the day!

Leader: No.

Schooner: No?

Leader: It was the queen and her faith in God who saved the lives of many people.

Schooner: You know what, boss?

Leader: Hmm?

Schooner: I'm glad when someone stands up for the little guy.

Leader: Me, too. And it's never easy.

Schooner: Especially when parrots do not-so-nice things to other parrots.

Leader: *(nods in agreement)*

Schooner: When that happens I try to step up to the plate.

Leader: The dinner plate?

Schooner: Very funny, boss.

Leader: Couldn't resist, birdie.

Schooner: I do like to eat!

Leader: *(nods)* I've seen your refrigerator.

Schooner: Grapes, sunflower seeds, chocolate chunks.

Leader: Let's get back to your point, Schooner.

Schooner: *(rambles)* Cheese chunks, peanut butter chunks, pineapple chunks.

Leader: Your point, Schooner?

Schooner: Oh, yes. I help my friends whenever I can.

Leader: *(hugs Schooner)* And that's what God wants us to do.

Schooner: Stand up and fly straight to shoo away evil. Shoo, evil, shoo!

Leader: I'll leave the flying to you. But yes to the rest!

Schooner: God defeats evil people.

Leader: We can help others.

Schooner: Good point, boss. How about hearing the whole story?

Leader: I like that plan! Bible 4U! up next.

Get ready to enjoy a story of bravery and courage. It has a King, a Queen, a hero and a villain. The story takes place at a time when the Jews had been captured and taken to another kingdom. Their captors could be cruel and just down right mean. Let me tell you about the daring characters in today's story.

First there is Cousin Mordecai, who is more than the Queen Esther's cousin. He adopted her after her parents died and is like a father to her. Mordecai is a hero who once saved the king's life.

Then we have Queen Esther. The king chose her from many women to be his queen. But she had a secret—she was a Jew. Last we have Hathach. He was the queen's servant and was very loyal to her. He played a small but important role that helped save a nation.

The queen trusted him to carry messages to and from her Uncle Mordecai. Give a listen as Hathach lets us in on the action.

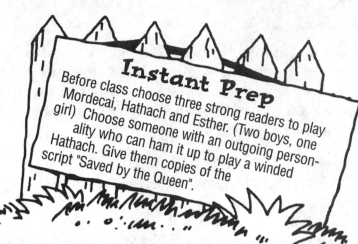

Instant Prep

Before class choose three strong readers to play Mordecai, Hathach and Esther. (Two boys, one girl) Choose someone with an outgoing personality who can ham it up to play a winded Hathach. Give them copies of the script "Saved by the Queen".

for Overachievers

Have a three-person drama team prepare the story. Dress them in Bible costumes. Drape Mordecai in a torn strip of burlap or torn brown craft paper and give Esther a crown, swatches of elegant fabric and costume jewelry. Use a bundle of cloth and a piece of paper for props.

Saved by the Queen
Based on the Book of Esther

Hathach comes center. Queen Esther is far stage left and Mordecai far stage right. Mordecai is crying melodramatically. He whimpers softly when Hathach begins.

Hathach: *(speaks to audience)* Poor Queen Esther, she has been worried. About what you ask? She has been worried about that. *(points to Mordecai)*

Mordecai: Waaaaaahh!

Hathach: Mordecai has ripped his clothes in sorrow and put on sackcloth and ashes to show his grief. All he does is cry and wail.

Mordecai: Waaaahh!

Queen Esther: Hathach, come here!

Hathach: *(goes to her)* Yes, my Queen.

Queen Esther: Take these clothes to Mordecai. Tell him to put them on instead of the sackcloth he's wearing.

Hathach: Yes, my lady. *(he hurries to Mordecai.)* Here are some clothes for you, Mordecai.

Mordecai: Waaahhhh! No *(sniff)* thank you *(sniff)*. Waaaahhhh!

Hathach: *(goes back to Queen)* He wouldn't take it, my lady.

Queen Esther: Go back and see if you can find out what's wrong.

Hathach: *(goes back to Mordecai)* Mordecai, the queen desires to know what's wrong.

Mordecai: The nasty nobleman, Haman, required all the people to bow down before him and I refused. That made Haman so furious that he planned to kill me.

Hathach: *(runs to Esther)* Haman told Mordecai to bow. He didn't. Haman is furious and wants to kill him.

Mordecai: *(calls across stage)* Wait! There's more.

Hathach runs back.

Mordecai: Haman's evil plan grew. He thought, "I won't kill just Haman—I'll kill all the Jewish people." He convinced the king that we're different and we don't obey the laws. Here's proof. *(hands him papers)* Give these papers to Queen Esther. Tell her to go to the king and beg for mercy for her people.

Hathach: *(goes to Queen)* Haman convinced the king to kill all the Jews. Here is the proof. *(hands her papers)* He wants you to go to the king and beg for mercy.

Queen Esther: I can't. No one can go to the king unless he invites her. It means death. The only exception is if the king holds out his scepter.

Hathach: *(runs to Mordecai)* She can't. Without an invitation, she could be killed.

Mordecai: I know. Tell her, "Don't think you will be spared because you are queen. You are still a Jew. Who knows? Maybe God put you there for such a time as this."

Hathach: *(runs back)* Being queen won't save you. Maybe God put you there for such a time as this.

Queen Esther: *(she thinks a moment)* Tell Mordecai to gather all the Jews to fast and pray for me for three days. I will do the same with my maids. When we finish, I will go to the king. And if I die, I die. *(she shrugs)*

Hathach: *(runs to Mordecai)* Gather all the Jews to fast and pray for her for three days. She will too and then she'll go to the king. If she dies, she dies. *(they both shrug and look worried)*

Mordecai and Queen Esther go down on their knees and pray. Hathach goes center and addresses audience.

Hathach: They prayed for three days, then Queen Esther went to the king. She'll tell you what happened.

Queen Esther: *(stands)* When I walked into the throne room without an invitation, every eye turned on me. My legs were shaking. The king saw me and I held my breath. I let out a big sigh of relief when he held out his scepter to let me know I was welcome. He asked, "What is it, Queen Esther? What is your request? Even up to half the kingdom, it will be granted to you." I invited the king to a banquet. Haman would be the only other guest.

Haman thought I was giving him a big honor. He had no idea that what I had in mind was to save my people. At the end of the meal I invited them to a second banquet. The king kept asking me what I wanted. Finally I asked the king to grant me my life and to spare the lives of my people. I explained that someone planned to kill us all. The king was furious and demanded to know who had done this. I pointed to Haman. He began to tremble with fear and beg for mercy.

Mordecai: *(stands)* The king had Haman hanged on the very gallows Haman had prepared for me. Then the king decreed that all Jews could defend themselves. It was a great victory for our people. We still celebrate it with the feast of Purim.

The three bow and exit.

Permission to photocopy this script granted for local church use. Copyright © Cook Communications Ministries.
Printed in Pick Up 'n' Do Lessons on Survivor Bible Style!

Queen Esther stepped up, took a big risk and saved her people. Approaching the king without an invitation meant putting her life on the line, but Queen Esther was up to the task. She knew that God had put her in a position to fight Haman and his evil plan.

Toss four numbered balls to different areas of the room. Invite the kids with the balls to come up front one-by-one and answer a question. Allow kids to get help from the group if they need it. After each correct answer, have kids drop their balls into a bag.

■ **What risk did Queen Esther take?**

■ **Why did Mordecai rip his clothes and put on ashes?**

■ **Suppose Esther had been too afraid to do anything. What might have happened?**

■ **Haman was an evil man with an evil plan. What kind of evil do we see today? How can we take a stand against it?**

Haman was so proud he thought everyone should bow to him. And he was a powerful man close to the king. He knew how to fool the king into doing what he wanted.

Esther was just a lovely young girl who was chosen to be queen. She didn't know that God put her in that position so that she could save his people. When the time came for her to act, she knew she would need God's help. So she and her maids and all the Jewish people went without eating and prayed for three days.

Queen Esther relied on God to guide and help her. God had her in the right place at the right time! And someday God may use you in that way. He may have you in just the right place to take a stand against evil. Remember Queen Esther and rely on God to help you! Today in your shepherd groups you'll make a cool game to show how the queen wins.

Dismiss kids to their shepherd groups.

Bible Verse
Do not be overcome by evil, but overcome evil with good.
Romans 12:21

② Shepherd's Spot

Gather your small group and help kids find the Book of Esther in their Bibles.

This whole book of the Bible is about the story we heard today. Queen Esther is a great heroine for God's people. Review the Bible story of Esther with your class.

■ **If you were a servant at the banquet where Esther told the king about Haman's evil plan, what would you tell your friends?**

■ **Can you imagine risking your life to save someone else? What would make you do that?**

Pass out the "And the Queen Wins!" handout. **This is a pretty fun game. When you put it together, you can have the queen knock out the bad guy, Haman.** Have kids cut out the circles. Ask a volunteer to read Romans 12:21 aloud: *"Do not be overcome by evil, but overcome evil with good."*

Help kids brainstorm and jot down on the appropriate circles evil things that happen in our world and how they can be a force for good. Have them assemble the circles according to the instructions on the handout. Encourage kids to retell the story by moving the figures.

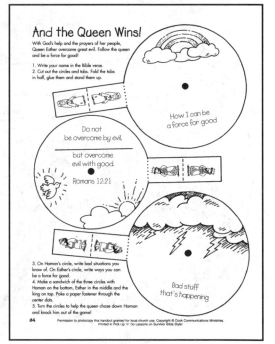

Let's pray about being a force for good against some of the evil things we talked about earlier. Dear Lord, thank you for the example of how Queen Esther helped her people survive. We pray for you to give us the courage to follow her example in facing evils such as (mention things kids named earlier). **We ask for the kind of wisdom and courage you gave Esther so that we can be your agents in our world. In Jesus' name, amen.**

Permission to photocopy this lesson page granted for local church use. Copyright © Cook Communications Ministries.
Printed in Pick Up 'n' Do Lessons on Survivor Bible Style!

And the Queen Wins!

With God's help and the prayers of her people, Queen Esther overcame great evil. Follow the queen and be a force for good!

1. Write your name in the Bible verse.
2. Cut out the circles and tabs. Fold the tabs in half, glue them and stand them up.

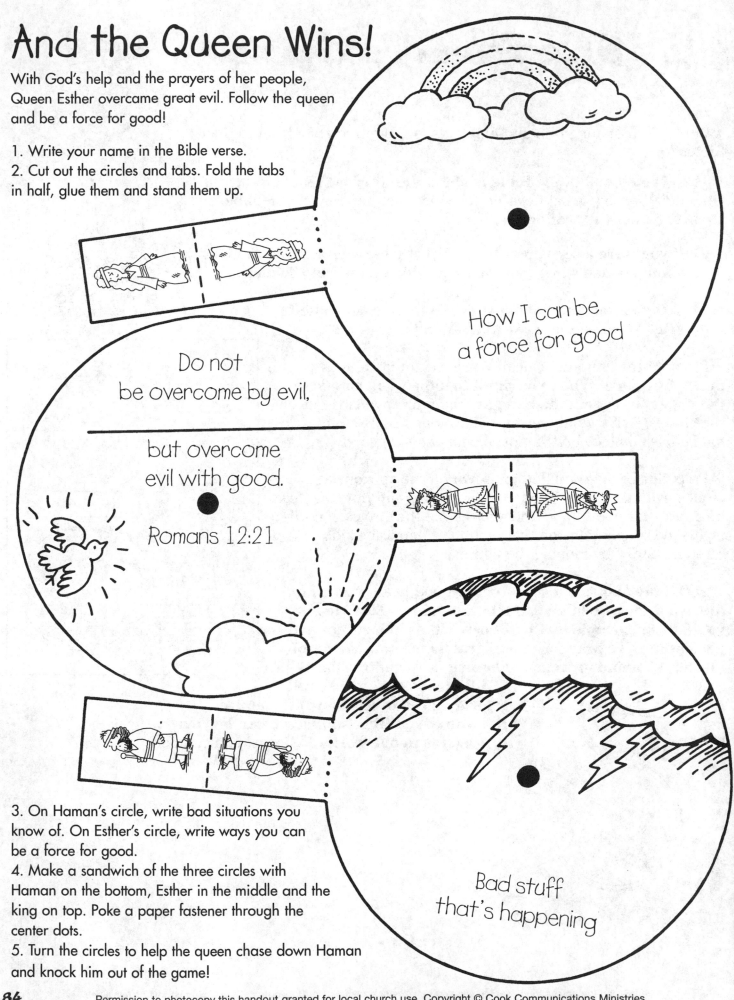

How I can be a force for good

Do not be overcome by evil,

_____

but overcome evil with good.

Romans 12:21

Bad stuff that's happening

3. On Haman's circle, write bad situations you know of. On Esther's circle, write ways you can be a force for good.
4. Make a sandwich of the three circles with Haman on the bottom, Esther in the middle and the king on top. Poke a paper fastener through the center dots.
5. Turn the circles to help the queen chase down Haman and knock him out of the game!

Permission to photocopy this handout granted for local church use. Copyright © Cook Communications Ministries.
Printed in Pick Up 'n' Do Lessons on Survivor Bible Style!

Workshop Wonders

Get List:
- [ ] small glass jars or plastic cups
- [ ] vegetable oil
- [ ] box of salt
- [ ] pitcher of water

God uses his people to change things. I hope you'll remember to be on the watch for ways to be a force for good this week. Remember to go about it like Queen Esther did—prayerfully, and relying on God's ever present help in time of need.

■ If you were going to make a movie of Queen Esther's story, which actor would you choose for the role of Esther? Haman? the king? Mordecai?

■ What Queen Ester did was not easy. She risked her life to speak to the king. Name one thing you did this week that was not easy but was the right thing to do.

■ How would you explain the word "evil"?

Let's do a cool experiment that demonstrates what happened in today's Bible story. People who live their lives for God make good things happen all around them. Their lives shine with the goodness of God's love. Have kids pour 1/2 inch of vegetable oil into their jars. **If you carefully hold your jar up to the light, you'll see how the oil sparkles and glistens.**

Then evil people come along. Their mean, selfish plans darken everything around them. Evil seems to rule the day. It can be frightening and discouraging. Remember how frightened and discouraged Mordecai and Esther were when they found out about Haman's evil plan? Have kids carefully pour a 1/4 inch layer of salt on top of the oil so it forms a thick crust.

But God has people like Queen Esther in place to be a force for good and conquer the evil. They move wisely and prayerfully into the situation. Show kids how to pour a stream of water carefully down the inside of the jar until it's almost full. Bubbles of oil will begin to break through the salt crust and rise to the surface.

God uses them to defeat evil and bring his goodness back to the top!

■ Can you tell about a time when you've seen good defeat evil?

■ What are the requirements for being someone God can use as a force for good?

Adapted from *Fun Science that Teaches God Word* by Mary Grace Becker and Susan Martins Miller.
Published by COOK COMMUNICATIONS MINISTRIES. Used by permission.
Permission to photocopy this lesson page granted for local church use. Copyright © Cook Communications Ministries.
Printed in Pick Up 'n' Do Lessons on Survivor Bible Style!

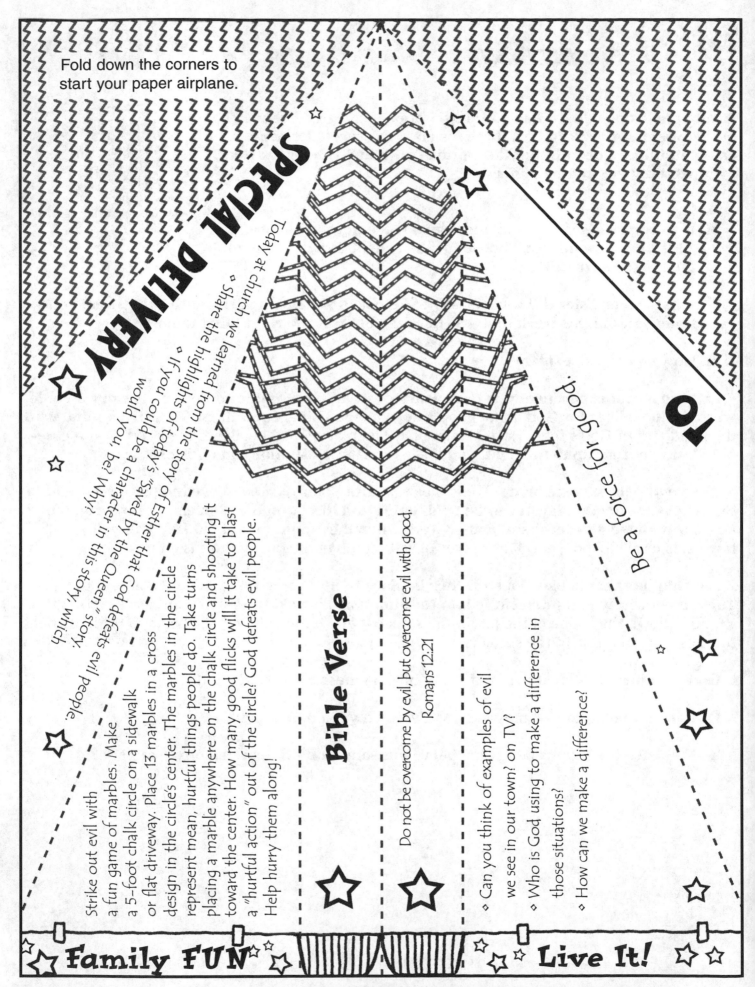

Fold down the corners to start your paper airplane.

SPECIAL DELIVERY

TO

Be a force for good.

Today at church we learned from the story of Esther that God defeats evil people.

Share the highlights of today's "Saved by the Queen" story, which—

If you could be a character in this story, would you be? Why?

Strike out evil with a fun game of marbles. Make a 5-foot chalk circle on a sidewalk or flat driveway. Place 13 marbles in a cross design in the circle's center. The marbles in the circle represent mean, hurtful things people do. Take turns placing a marble anywhere on the chalk circle and shooting it toward the center. How many good flicks will it take to blast a "hurtful action" out of the circle? God defeats evil people. Help hurry them along!

Bible Verse

Do not be overcome by evil, but overcome evil with good.
Romans 12:21

◊ Can you think of examples of evil we see in our town? on TV?

◊ Who is God using to make a difference in those situations?

◊ How can we make a difference?

☆ Family FUN ☆   Live It! ☆

Permission to photocopy this handout granted for local church use. Copyright © Cook Communications Ministries.
Printed in Pick Up 'n' Do Lessons on Survivor Bible Style!

Way Cool

Option

Get Set
LARGE GROUP ■ Greet kids and do a puppet skit. Schooner's small hurt leads to a discussion on three faith-filled men and a furnace of fire.

❏ large bird puppet   ❏ puppeteer

1

Bible 4U! Instant Drama
LARGE GROUP ■ Meet three big-time survivors: Shadrach, Meshach and Abednego. Witness their captivity by Enemy #1, King Nebuchadnezzar.

❏ 2 actors   ❏ copies of pp. 90-91, Flame Out! script   ❏ 4 numbered balls
Optional: ❏ soldier's uniforms   ❏ swords, helmets   ❏ brick furnace back drop
❏ red, yellow and orange crepe paper streamers   ❏ fan

2

Shepherd's Spot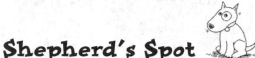
SMALL GROUP ■ Use the "Watchin' Over You!" handout as a visual reminder of the promise in Psalm 34:7 that angels guard God's people.

❏ Bibles   ❏ pencils   ❏ scissors   ❏ copies of p. 94, Watchin' Over You!   ❏ copies of p. 96, Special Delivery

Option

Workshop Wonders
SMALL GROUP ■ Sculpt a trio of angels from clay; have them surround "worry flames."

❏ self-hardening clay   ❏ waxed paper   ❏ yellow and orange construction paper
❏ pencils   ❏ zip-top bags

Bible Basis
Fiery Furnace.
Daniel 3:1, 4–6,
19, 20, 24–28

Learn It!
God delivers those who trust in him.

Live It!
Don't worry about God's enemies.

Bible Verse
The angel of the LORD encamps around those who fear him, and he delivers them. Psalm 34:7

Quick Takes

Daniel 3:1, 4–6, 19, 20 24–28

3:1 King Nebuchadnezzar made an image of gold, ninety feet high and nine feet wide, and set it up on the plain of Dura in the province of Babylon.
4 Then the herald loudly proclaimed, "This is what you are commanded to do, O peoples, nations and men of every language:
5 As soon as you hear the sound of the horn, flute, zither, lyre, harp, pipes and all kinds of music, you must fall down and worship the image of gold that King Nebuchadnezzar has set up.
6 Whoever does not fall down and worship will immediately be thrown into a blazing furnace."
19 Then Nebuchadnezzar was furious with Shadrach, Meshach and Abednego, and his attitude towards them changed. He ordered the furnace to be heated seven times hotter than usual
20 and commanded some of the strongest soldiers in his army to tie up Shadrach, Meshach and Abednego and throw them into the blazing furnace.
24 Then King Nebuchadnezzar leaped to his feet in amazement and asked his advisers, "Weren't there three men that we tied up and threw into the fire?" They replied, "Certainly, O king."
25 He said, "Look! I see four men walking around in the fire, unbound and unharmed, and the fourth looks like a son of the gods."
26 Nebuchadnezzar then approached the opening of the blazing furnace and shouted, "Shadrach, Meshach and Abednego, servants of the Most High God, come out! Come here!" So Shadrach, Meshach and Abednego came out of the fire,
28 Then Nebuchadnezzar said, "Praise be to the God of Shadrach, Meshach and Abednego, who has sent his angel and rescued his servants! They trusted in him and defied the king's command and were willing to give up their lives rather than serve or worship any god except their own God."

Insights

Throughout the centuries devout Jews encountered trouble by refusing to bow to anyone other than God. In accordance with the second of the Ten Commandments, God's people would not make or bow down to an idol. So when King Nebuchadnezzar ordered everyone to bow to his 90-foot golden statue, Shadrach, Meshach and Abednego "took a stand" as conscientious objectors.

Nebuchadnezzar was no petty ruler to contend with. He is best remembered for the marvels of his capitol city of Babylon, near modern-day Baghdad. At that time it was the largest city in the world, noted for its hanging gardens and magnificent city wall and gates. The most powerful monarch of the Chaldean line, Nebuchadnezzar united the empires of Babylonia and Media by marriage. Such a powerful, absolute monarch did not take the defiance of the Jews lightly.

He gave Shadrach, Meshach and Abednego one last chance to bow to his image. Their in-your-face refusal was stunning. "The God we serve is able to save us…and even if he does not, we want you to know, O king, that we will not serve your gods."

Despite the king's rage and a furnace heated seven times hotter than usual, Shadrach, Meshach and Abednego stayed cool—literally—in God's care. Use their calm, courageous example to encourage kids not to fear God's enemies, but to trust in his amazing ability to protect them.

Get Set

Open with lively music, then greet the kids. **Today's hot furnace Bible story is one of the most amazing survivor stories in the Bible. God's enemies are no match for him! God delivers those who trust in him. Schooner, fly up and say hello.** *Schooner pops up.*

Leader: Good to see you again, my lil' parrot.

Schooner: Ouch!

Leader: What's the matter, Schooner?

Schooner: I burned my beak on a cup of tea.

Leader: Sorry you have a boo-boo today.

Schooner: Me too.

Leader: There's something I do with my *(son, daughter, niece)* when *(he)* she has a hurt.

Schooner: What's that?

Leader: I kiss it and make it better.

Schooner: *(looks at the group)* Um. That won't be necessary.

Leader: I wish I could help in some way.

Schooner: Every time I open my beak to speak it hurts.

Leader: I know the cure!

Schooner: What's that, boss?

Leader: Don't speak.

Schooner: It doesn't hurt that much. OUCH! Yes it does! Yes it does!

Leader: Try humming.

Schooner: Humming?

Leader: Yes.

Schooner: How will you understand me?

Leader: I think I know you well enough, Schooner.

Schooner: *(nods head in agreement)*

Leader: Today's Bible story is amazing. It's hard to know where to start.

Schooner: Hummmmmmmmmm.

Leader: At the beginning? Okay. God saves three faith-filled men from the fiery flames of a blazing furnace.

Schooner: Hummmmmmmmm.

Leader: Because they refused to bow down to the king's golden statue.

Schooner: Hummmmmmmmmm.

Leader: No, they didn't turn into crispy critters. As a matter of fact, their hair wasn't singed and they didn't even smell like smoke.

Schooner: Hummmmmmmmm.

Leader: How can that happen? Only God can provide that kind of protection!

Schooner: Hummmmmm.

Leader: I know—you got burned by a cup of tea and they didn't get burned at all in the middle of a blazing furnace. Maybe next time you should try lemonade.

Schooner: Hummmmmmmm.

Leader: Well, I think God was teaching ol' King Nebuchadnezzar a lesson.

Schooner: King Nebucha-WHAT?

Leader: Nebuchadnezzar. The king of a huge empire.

Schooner: Hummmmmmm.

Leader: I agree. Putting people into a furnace is not a nice thing to do. But this king was so powerful he could do anything he wanted.

Schooner: Hummmmmmm.

Leader: No, I wouldn't want to have him for my enemy either. But God is in charge. We don't need to be afraid of anyone.

Schooner: Hummmmmmm.

Leader: Nope. We don't need to fear anyone at all. God delivers those who trust in him. You know, you're really good at this humming thing, Schooner. Why don't you consider doing it all the time?

Schooner: Because I'm not a hummingbird. I'm just a parrot with a singed beak. But I'm glad those guys in the story didn't get singed.

Leader: Really.

Schooner: They kept their cool.

Leader: Uh-huh.

Schooner: I'd like to know more about them.

Leader: Hum.

Schooner: Very funny. Bible 4U! up next.

Permission to photocopy this script granted for local church use. Copyright © Cook Communications Ministries.
Printed in Pick Up 'n' Do Lessons on Survivor Bible Style!

1 Bible 4U!

Welcome to today's thrilling episode of Bible 4U! Theater—it's going to be a hot one! You'll meet three big-time survivors: Shadrach, Meshach and Abednego. These guys are followers of the one true God who have been taken captive by their enemy, King Nebuchadnezzar. The king doesn't worship God, but he knows bright guys when he sees them. And even though he has captured Shadrach, Meshach and Abednego along with the rest of God's people, he ends up putting them in charge of part of his kingdom. Smart move!

Instant Prep

You'll need two people to play the roles of Bubba and Moose. Choose good readers from your class who can act "buff and tough." Your actors will need copies of the "Flame Out!" script below.

for Overachievers

Dress Moose and Bubba in soldier's tunics. Outfit them with swords and helmets. Create a backdrop that suggests a large brick furnace. Add crepe paper "flames" and blow them with a hidden fan.

Unfortunately, the king also makes a move that's not so smart. He builds a giant golden statue and forces everybody to worship it. Shadrach, Meshach and Abednego don't want to worship the statue. They know that to refuse means they'll be put to death. But they love the Lord their God so much that they wouldn't think of worshiping some statue. They decide to continue worshiping God and take the consequences for disobeying the king. When they do, something amazing happens. You'll hear about it from Moose and Bubba, two strong soldiers in King Nebuchadnezzar's army.

Flame Out!
Based on Daniel 3:1, 4–6, 19, 20, 24–28

Bubba: *(to audience)* Hey there. I'm Bubba. And this is my buddy Moose.

Moose: We're two of the strongest soldiers in King Nebechudnezzar's army.

Bubba: And nobody…

Moose: …but nobody…

Bubba: …messes with us when we're working.

Moose: If we tell you to do something…

Bubba: You'd better do it. And if we put you in jail…

Moose: …you stay in jail. And if we say, "jump!"…

Bubba: …you say, "how high?"

Moose: And if we throw you into the fiery furnace…

Bubba: *(elbows Moose in the ribs—gently!—and stage whispers)* Shhh! That's kind of a sore spot, remember?

Moose: Oh yeah.

Bubba: You see, it's all on account of these three Hebrew guys.

Moose: Yeah. What were their names again…Shake-the-bed, Make-the-bed and To-bed-we-go?

Bubba: Uh, close. Try Shadrach, Meshach and Abednego. They ruined our perfect track record.

Moose: Or rather, their God did.

Bubba: It all started when King Nebuchadnezzar built a giant gold statue and told all the people of the kingdom to bow down and worship it.

Moose: When the king gives a command, you don't ask questions.

Bubba: There were three heads sticking out of the crowd.

Moose: Ya see, these guys were so committed to their God that they refused to bow down.

Bubba: That's right. They refused! We couldn't believe it. We figured they were either crazy or…or…or outta their minds.

Moose: So the king called them to stand before him. And he told them again to bow down to the statue or else he'd throw them into the fiery furnace.

Bubba: They said, "We won't bow down. Our God can save us, but even if he doesn't, we want you to know we won't bow down."

Moose: They weren't afraid of the king at all! As you might expect, that made the king even more angry.

Bubba: You could say he was pretty hot under the collar.

Moose: So he told us soldiers to go make the fiery furnace seven times hotter than usual.

Bubba: Man, was it scorching hot! I could hardly stand being near it.

Moose: Then some of our buddies led Shadrach, Meshach and Abednego out to the furnace.

Bubba: You'll never believe what happened…

Moose: The fire was so hot that it burned up the soldiers!

Bubba: Boy am I glad it wasn't our job to throw Shadrach, Meshach and Abednego in there. We wouldn't have survived.

Moose: But Shadrach, Meshach and Abednego did.

Bubba: They not only made it into the furnace alive…they were actually walking around in there!

Moose: It was strange. They were walking around, but their feet weren't burning.

Bubba: Their clothes weren't burning.

Moose: Their hair wasn't burning.

Bubba: They were just, like, totally cool!

Moose: And here's what was even stranger…While we were watching them in there, another person just appeared out of nowhere.

Bubba: Three guys got thrown in there, but there were definitely four walking around.

Moose: The fourth guy looked like an angel or something. We were really weirded out.

Bubba: King Nebuchadnezzar must have been weirded out too, because he told us to get those guys out of there, quick! He was amazed by Shadrach, Meshach and Abednego.

Moose: And by their God.

Bubba: He forgot about his statue pretty quickly.

Moose: The king saw how God saved these men's lives, and he gave a new command. He told all the people of the kingdom that anyone who said anything bad about the God of Shadrach, Meshach and Abednego would be punished. From now on, I'm going to bow down to their God.

(Bubba and Moose exit)

Permission to photocopy this script granted for local church use. Copyright © Cook Communications Ministries.
Printed in Pick Up 'n' Do Lessons on Survivor Bible Style!

Wow! That's some story, isn't it? I'm sweating just thinking about it! Let's show our appreciation for Moose and Bubba. Now, who thinks they're hot at answering questions today? Toss the four numbered balls to different parts of the room.

Stand up if you have ball#1. Bring the kids with the balls to the front one by one and ask these questions. Allow kids to get help from the group if they need it. After each correct answer, let kids drop their balls into a bag.

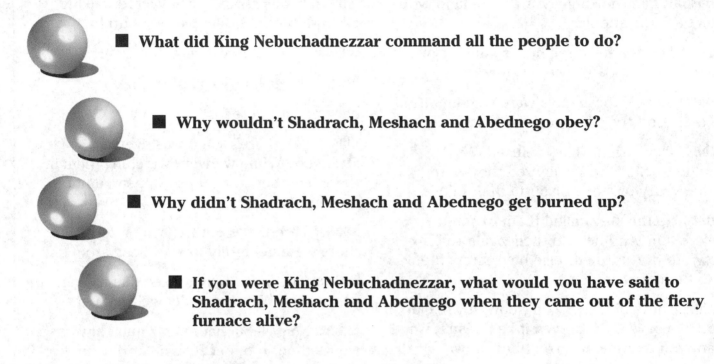

■ **What did King Nebuchadnezzar command all the people to do?**

■ **Why wouldn't Shadrach, Meshach and Abednego obey?**

■ **Why didn't Shadrach, Meshach and Abednego get burned up?**

■ **If you were King Nebuchadnezzar, what would you have said to Shadrach, Meshach and Abednego when they came out of the fiery furnace alive?**

Way to go! You sure remember a lot about today's story. Isn't God amazing? Shadrach, Meshach and Abednego thought so too—and that was before God rescued them from the fiery furnace. They trusted that God would take care of them, even if they didn't know exactly how he would do it. You know what? Today, we serve the same God who delivered Shadrach, Meshach and Abednego. And that means he can help us, too.

In fact, Psalm 34:7 tells us that "The angel of the LORD encamps around those who fear him, and he delivers them." Do you know what it means to fear God? It doesn't mean that you're scared. It just means that you have respect for his mighty power. Today in your shepherd groups, you'll have fun learning more about our great God and how he rescues his people.

Bible Verse
The angel of the LORD encamps around those who fear him, and he delivers them.
Psalm 34:7

Dismiss kids to their shepherd groups.

Gather your small group and help kids find Daniel 3 in their Bibles.

The book of Daniel tells us about some of the things that happened to God's people when they were captives in Babylon. Although they were captives, they got put in charge of important business. But because they believed in God, they weren't willing to go along with everything that happened in their new land. Let's have a look at their story.

Have volunteers take turns reading 3:1, 4–6, 19, 20, 24–28

Angels are real, and I don't mean just on top of your Christmas tree! Throughout the Bible we hear about angels helping, protecting, and giving messages from God. Let's make angels to remind you that God's guardians are watching over you! Have kids cut out and assemble the "Watchin' Over You!" handout according to the instructions.

■ **If you were in a scary spot, what person would you choose to have with you?**

■ **How is having angels around you even better than that?**

I hope you'll hang your angel in a place where it will remind you that God can take care of you in any situation. Before we finish today, let's pray for people who need God's protection. Let kids mention people they'd like to pray for. Then close with prayer. **Dear Lord, sometimes obeying you makes us stand out from the crowd. And that can be scary. Help us remember that you can take care of us in any situation—even a fiery furnace! We ask your protection for** (mention kids' concerns). **Thank you for your help and for watching over us. In Jesus' name, amen.**

Watchin' Over You!

A heavenly figure appeared in the fiery furnace with Shadrach, Meshach and Abednego. You may not see them, but this verse assures you that an angel of the Lord watches over you, too!

1. Cut out the angel and the wings.

2. Line up the second set of wings behind the angel. Push brads through the dots at the shoulders.

3. Bend a straw in the middle. Punch holes one-half inch from each end of the straw and through the dots on the wing tips. Fasten brads through the holes.

4. Use the straw as a hanger. Move it up and down to make the angel fly!

The angel of the LORD encamps around those who fear him, and he delivers them. Psalm 34:7

94

Permission to photocopy this handout granted for local church use. Copyright © Cook Communications Ministries. Printed in Pick Up 'n' Do Lessons on Survivor Bible Style!

Permission to photocopy this lesson page granted for local church use. Copyright © Cook Communications Ministries.
Printed in Pick Up 'n' Do Lessons on Survivor Bible Style!

Watchin' Over You!

A heavenly figure appeared in the fiery furnace with Shadrach, Meshach and Abednego. You may not see them, but this verse assures you that an angel of the Lord watches over you, too!

The angel of the LORD encamps around those who fear him, and he delivers them. Psalm 34:7

1. Cut out the angel and the wings.

2. Line up the second set of wings behind the angel. Push brads through the dots at the shoulders.

3. Bend a straw in the middle. Punch holes one-half inch from each end of the straw and through the dots on the wing tips. Fasten brads through the holes.

4. Use the straw as a hanger. Move it up and down to make the angel fly!

Permission to photocopy this handout granted for local church use. Copyright © Cook Communications Ministries. Printed in Pick Up 'n' Do Lessons on Survivor Bible Style!

Today your kids will make a trio of angels (or more if they'd like!) that surround flames filled with worries and scary situations. Make a sample craft before class as an example for your kids.

Get List:
- ❑ self-hardening clay
- ❑ waxed paper
- ❑ yellow and orange construction paper
- ❑ pencils
- ❑ zip-top bags

Shadrach, Meshach and Abednego did a super job of keeping the heat off in today's story! I'm not sure I would have been so brave!

■ **How were Shadrach, Meshach and Abednego able to stand up to the king even when they knew it meant receiving a death sentence?**

When we put God first in our lives and obey him in everything, we're bound to run into enemies. But they're God's enemies, not our enemies, and we can trust God to handle them! Hold up your sample angels. **This trio of angels shows us what God does for us.** Have a volunteer read Psalm 34:7 aloud: *"The angel of the LORD encamps around those who fear him, and he delivers them."*

Think for a moment about times when it might be scary to take a stand as a follower of God like Shadrach, Meshach and Abednego did in today's story. Tear little flames of construction paper and write those fearful situations on the flames. Encourage ideas such as refusing to let someone copy homework, reporting a friend who's shoplifting or standing up for their beliefs to a teacher who doesn't believe in God. After kids have written on their flames, encourage them to share what they wrote. Let them curl the flames gently around a pencil.

It's wonderful to know that God sends his angels to guard us in those situations. Take a piece of clay and build your own trio of angels. When you've finished, place your "fearful flames" inside their circle of protection.

Hand out zip-top bags so kids can take their clay creations with them.

At home, place your angels in a sunny spot and let them dry. Remember, obeying God means that you'll run into enemies sometimes. But God can deliver you and take care of you.

Permission to photocopy this lesson page granted for local church use. Copyright © Cook Communications Ministries.
Printed in Pick Up 'n' Do Lessons on Survivor Bible Style!

Fold down the corners to
start your paper airplane.

SPECIAL DELIVERY

Today at church we learned from the story of Shadrach, Meshach and Abednego that God delivers those who trust in him. Share a spectacular highlight of this amazing Bible story with your parents. (Shadrach, Meshach and Abednego were thrown in a furnace but did not burn!)

TO

◇ God delivers those who trust in him.
◇ Don't worry about God's enemies.

Bible Verse

The angel of the LORD encamps around those who fear him, and he delivers them.

Psalm 34:7

Furnaces, like campfires, are meant to help people, not hurt them. Make this delicious snack the next time you and your family gather around the fire. Peel back one side of a ripe banana. Use a plastic knife to cut away the banana's center. Sprinkle the open space with chocolate chunks and mini-marshmallows. Close the skin and wrap the banana in aluminum foil. Ask an adult to place the treat in the hot coals for about three minutes. As you enjoy your snack, remember that God can help you take the heat!

◇ What do you think God wants you to learn from this spectacular survivor story?
◇ Tell about a time you obeyed God even though it meant someone got angry with you.

Family FUN

Live It!

Permission to photocopy this handout granted for local church use. Copyright © Cook Communications Ministries.
Printed in Pick Up 'n' Do Lessons on Survivor Bible Style!

The Not-So-Hungry Lions

Get Set
LARGE GROUP ■ Greet kids and do a puppet skit. Lions make a house call in Schooner's puppet script.

❏ large bird puppet ❏ puppeteer

1

Bible 4U! Instant Drama
LARGE GROUP ■ Hear about Daniel's faithfulness to God in this Bible story script.

❏ 3 actors ❏ copies of pp. 100-101, The Satraps' Sly Trap script ❏ 4 numbered balls
Optional: ❏ Persian tunic and belt ❏ face paint ❏ fur or paper cat ears ❏ braided yarn cat tails ❏ plants ❏ colorful pillows ❏ vases

2

Shepherd's Spot
SMALL GROUP ■ Use the "Well, Shut My Mouth!" handout to help kids remember that God will protect those who are faithful to him.

❏ Bibles ❏ pencils ❏ scissors ❏ copies of p. 104, Well, Shut My Mouth! ❏ copies of p. 106, Special Delivery

Workshop Wonders
SMALL GROUP ■ Make and gobble up fun and tasty lion treats.

❏ paper plates ❏ canned pear halves ❏ chow mien noodles ❏ raisins ❏ Bugles® crackers ❏ aerosol cream cheese spread ❏ spoons

Bible Basis
Daniel 6:3–5, 7, 9–11, 13, 14, 16, 17, 19–23, 25, 26

Learn It!
God watches over us.

Live It!
Be faithful to God.

Bible Verse
For the LORD loves the just and will not forsake his faithful ones. They will be protected forever.
Psalm 37:28

Daniel 6:3–5, 7, 9–11, 13, 14, 16, 17, 19–21, 25, 26

6:3 Now Daniel so distinguished himself among the administrators and the satraps by his exceptional qualities that the king planned to set him over the whole kingdom.

4 At this, the administrators and the satraps tried to find grounds for charges against Daniel in his conduct of government affairs, but they were unable to do so. They could find no corruption in him, because he was trustworthy and neither corrupt nor negligent.

5 Finally these men said, "We will never find any basis for charges against this man Daniel unless it has something to do with the law of his God."

7 The royal administrators, prefects, satraps, advisers and governors have all agreed that the king should issue an edict and enforce the decree that anyone who prays to any god or man during the next thirty days, except to you, O king, shall be thrown into the lions' den.

9 So King Darius put the decree in writing.

10 Now when Daniel learned that the decree had been published, he went home to his upstairs room where the windows opened towards Jerusalem. Three times a day he got down on his knees and prayed, giving thanks to his God, just as he had done before.

11 Then these men went as a group and found Daniel praying and asking God for help.

13 Then they said to the king, "Daniel, who is one of the exiles from Judah, pays no attention to you, O king, or to the decree you put in writing. He still prays three times a day."

14 When the king heard this, he was greatly distressed; he was determined to rescue Daniel and made every effort until sundown to save him.

16 So the king gave the order, and they brought Daniel and threw him into the lions' den. The king said to Daniel, "May your God, whom you serve continually, rescue you!"

17 A stone was brought and placed over the mouth of the den, and the king sealed it with his own signet ring and with the rings of his nobles, so that Daniel's situation might not be changed.

19 At the first light of dawn, the king got up and hurried to the lions' den.

20 When he came near the den, he called to Daniel in an anguished voice, "Daniel, servant of the living God, has your God, whom you serve continually, been able to rescue you from the lions?"

21 Daniel answered, "O king, live forever!

22 My God sent his angel, and he shut the mouths of the lions. They have not hurt me, because I was found innocent in his sight. Nor have I ever done any wrong before you, O king."

23 The king was overjoyed and gave orders to lift Daniel out of the den. And when Daniel was lifted from the den, no wound was found on him, because he had trusted in his God.

25 Then King Darius wrote to all the peoples, nations and men of every language throughout the land: "May you prosper greatly!

26 I issue a decree that in every part of my kingdom people must fear and reverence the God of Daniel. For he is the living God and he endures forever; his kingdom will not be destroyed, his dominion will never end."

Insights

Jealousy drives the plot of this story. Daniel did such a good job as an administrator that King Darius planned to promote him over all the others. But he lived such a godly life that his detractors were hard pressed to find grounds to accuse him. Finally they struck on it—a ban on praying to anyone but the king.

This clever plot played into the king's vanity. Without realizing it, he signed away Daniel's life—or so the plotters thought. The king could not revoke a law he had signed. So just before he regretfully sealed the stone covering the lions' den, he wished God's care for his faithful servant. After a sleepless night he hurried to lions' den to find Daniel alive and well. With Daniel out, the king threw in the plotters and suddenly the lions' appetites returned!

Jesus himself said, "In this world you will have trouble" (John 16:33). How wonderful to be able to trust the end result to God! Use this lesson to teach kids to focus on being faithful to God and let God take care of the rest.

Get Set

Option

Open with lively music, then greet the kids. **We have an amazing Bible survivor story to share today. A cave of hungry lions is all the hint I will give for now! We'll learn that God watches over his faithful people. Schooner, pop up and join us.** *Schooner pops up.*

Schooner: Present and accounted for, boss.

Leader: At ease, Schooner.

Schooner: Yes sir!

Leader: To start our time together I'd like to play a word game.

Schooner: I'm game! Ha. Get it? You said game. And I said game.

Leader: Yes. I get it.

Schooner: *Squawk!*

Leader: I'll say three words. You fill in the blank. Okay?

Schooner: You're the boss.

Leader: Here goes…eeny…meeny…miney…

Schooner: Me!

Leader: I was thinking of the word Mo.

Schooner: Eeny…Meeny…Miney…Mo? "Me" sounds better, boss.

Leader: Mo is the name of the new baby giraffe at the zoo.

Schooner: Cute!

Leader: I've heard the baby giraffe is teeny-tiny.

Schooner: Eeny…Meeny…Miney…Teeny…Tiny …Mo!

Leader: Great name, Schooner!

Schooner: You know, I have an aunt and uncle who live at the zoo.

Leader: Sounds like a good place to retire.

Schooner: It's affordable.

Leader: And all their meals are taken care of.

Schooner: Right! So why all this talk about animals?

Leader: Lions are the thing in today's Bible story.

Schooner: I think this is a first for us.

Leader: You're right, Schooner. We've never talked about lions before.

Schooner: Is this a musical Bible story where lions sing and dance?

Leader: Afraid not, Schooner.

Schooner: A wild kingdom special?

Leader: Nope.

Schooner: Okay, boss. Let's get something straight.

Leader: Yes?

Schooner: Does this story have happy…or hungry lions?

Leader: Hungry.

Schooner: I don't think I want to hear anymore!

Leader: It's a true survivor story, Schooner. Daniel, the man in today's story, loves to pray to God.

Schooner: So where's the problem?

Leader: The officials of the day wanted Daniel to worship their king instead.

Schooner: Old Testament know-it-alls!

Leader: Now, now, Schooner.

Schooner: *(ruffles feathers)* Why do the high-and-mighty wise guys always mess things up?

Leader: Because kings and rulers like to be in charge.

Schooner: So what happens to our praying Daniel?

Leader: I don't want to give it all away here, Schooner.

Schooner: A hint, pleeeeeeese?

Leader: Let's just say the story has a happy survivor ending.

Schooner: I knew it! God watches over us.

Leader: Let's be faithful to our faithful God.

Schooner: *Squawk!* Roar! *Squawk!* Roar!

Leader: You sound like a squeaky door, Schooner.

Schooner: Talent, boss. It's hard to come by.

Leader: Bible 4U! up next.

Permission to photocopy this script granted for local church use. Copyright © Cook Communications Ministries.
Printed in Pick Up 'n' Do Lessons on Survivor Bible Style!

1 Bible 4U!

Welcome to Bible 4U Theatre. Get ready for a roaring good time as we hear about Daniel's faithfulness to God! Many years before our story, Jerusalem was conquered by a Persian king. Israelite captives, including Daniel, were taken back to Babylon as slaves. Even though Daniel was a captive in the land we know today as Iraq, he knew God was with him. God helped Daniel grow in wisdom and abilities. Daniel praised God and trusted his plan.

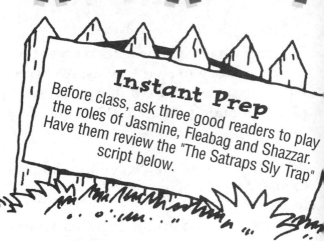

Instant Prep
Before class, ask three good readers to play the roles of Jasmine, Fleabag and Shazzar. Have them review the "The Satraps Sly Trap" script below.

As our story opens, we find Daniel no longer a slave but one of the most powerful men in the kingdom. He is one of three supervisors over 120 satraps. Daniel has become a favorite of the king because he is trustworthy and wise. The king has decided to promote Daniel over all the other supervisors and governors, called satraps, of the kingdom. Trouble is brewing—powerful plotting by jealous fellas, faithful praying from a believing heart, a duped king powerless to change his own decree, and roaring lions that become gentle as kittens. And you have prime seats with a great view on all the action as a couple of cool cats let us in on the scoop from the castle.
Now for a tale of tails!

for Overachievers
Glue construction paper ears to headbands for Jasmine and Fleabag. Make whiskers with face paint and braid yarn for tails. Make a tunic for Shazzar by draping a large rectangle of material around him and tying it with a colorful belt. Create a lush Persian setting with plants, colorful pillows and tall vases.

The Satrap's Sly Trap
Based on Daniel 6:3–5, 7, 9–11, 13, 14, 16, 17, 19–23, 25, 26

Jasmine: Meooow me to introduce myself – I'm Jasmine, the castle cat. My master's King Darius of Babylon in Purrrrsia.

Fleabag: You can call me Fleabag. I was a stray until my master Daniel took me in. I'm a pretty lucky kitty, because Daniel is one of the most important men in the kingdom.

Jasmine: Have we got a tale for you!

Fleabag: This story will curl your whiskers.

Jasmine: It started one night when I was patrolling the castle. I overheard one of the sneakiest people in the kingdom, Shazzar the Satrap.

Fleabag: *(looking around suspiciously)* Cat trap? Where?

Jasmine: No, no, not cat trap. Satrap. That's what they call the governors. Anyway I overheard Shazzar the Satrap and the other governors plotting.

Shazzar: *(enters on the opposite side)* Daniel has got to go! He was a slave and now the king's planning to put him in charge of the whole kingdom! He'll be our boss. I'm not about to let that happen! *(stomps off)*

Fleabag: So there you have it. Daniel was one of three supervisors over the satraps. Daniel did his work so well that King Darius planned to put him over all the supervisors and satraps. Top dog in the kingdom, so to speak.

Jasmine: *Puh-leeze.*

Fleabag: Sorry. I meant coolest cat in the kingdom. But wait, that would be you, right?

Jasmine: *Rrrrrrrrr!*

Fleabag: Shazzar and the other satraps watched Daniel every minute, waiting to pounce at the slightest excuse. But Daniel never did anything wrong!

Jasmine: So, the satraps set their trap.

Fleabag: *(whispers loudly)* Shh! There's Shazzar again. I think he's about to let the cat out of the bag!

Shazzar: *(enters pacing)* OK, we'll never be able to accuse Daniel of anything unless it has something to do with his God. He prays faithfully every day. Not just once or twice, but three times a day without fail! Hmmmm…

Fleabag: Boy, you can almost hear the trap door.

Shazzar: *(snaps fingers)* That's it! We'll trick the king into issuing an order saying no one in the kingdom can pray to anyone except the king for 30 days. Anyone who disobeys the order will be thrown into the lions' den. Since the king cannot change an order once it's signed, he won't be able to help Daniel! We've got him now! *(exits rubbing hands together)*

Jasmine: That's exactly what the satraps did! The king fell for their plan hook, line and sinker!

Fleabag: *(interrupts)* Yum. Fish—it's what's for dinner!

Jasmine: They were sure they had Daniel right where they wanted him.

Fleabag: And they did—on his knees! Everyone knows Daniel is faithful to God no matter what!

Jasmine: Ever wonder why Daniel loves God enough to risk being a lion snack?

Fleabag: I don't have to wonder. I know! Our carpet is worn out where he kneels to pray.

Jasmine: What does he pray about?

Fleabag: Everything! Daniel knows God loves him and he knows that God is in control. I hear him praising God for his faithfulness every day.

Fleabag: Shazzar and the others didn't have to wait long to catch Daniel on his knees praying to God. Daniel didn't even try to hide. He prayed right in his window!

Jasmine: King Darius felt terrible that he couldn't keep Daniel from being thrown to the big cats! At sundown they sealed Daniel in the lions' den.

Fleabag: I was so afraid for Daniel that my paws were shaking, my tail was twitching and half my fur fell out.

Jasmine: King Darius felt the same way. He didn't eat or sleep all night. The minute the sun came up, he rushed to the lions' den.

Fleabag: King Darius yelled, "Daniel, servant of the living God! Has your God saved you from the lions?"

Jasmine: Daniel answered, "God sent his angel to shut the lions' mouths. They have not hurt me."

Fleabag: Well, shut my mouth!

Jasmine: Like that'll ever happen!

Fleabag: So the king had Daniel pulled from the lions' den and there wasn't a mark on him!

Jasmine: And the satraps ended up in their own trap. The king had them thrown in the den. And this time the lions were hungry. Then King Darius made another law that could not be changed. A good law this time!

Fleabag: He proclaimed that everyone in his kingdom must fear and respect the true God who rescued Daniel from the lions.

Jasmine: God's plan worked purrfectly. He watched over Daniel and the bad guys ended up in the soup, so to speak.

Fleabag: And Daniel was home in time to feed me breakfast!

Jasmine: Do you ever stop thinking about food?

Fleabag: Nope. Wanna go snooping around for a snack?

Jasmine: Why not? Yum! Got any juicy mice on special around here?

They exit.

Permission to photocopy this script granted for local church use. Copyright © Cook Communications Ministries.

Imagine a sleepover with lions! A narrow escape, for sure. Let's see if this story made purrr-fect sense to you!

Toss the four numbered balls to different parts of the room. Bring the kids with the balls to the front one-by-one and ask these questions. Allow kids to get help from the group if they need it. After each correct answer, let kids drop their balls into a bag.

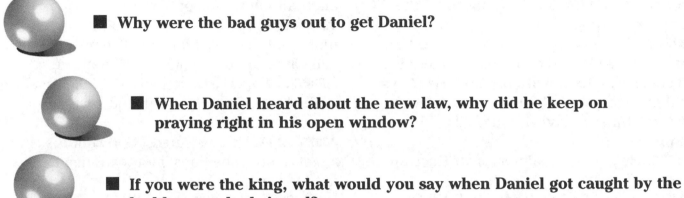

■ Why were the bad guys out to get Daniel?

■ When Daniel heard about the new law, why did he keep on praying right in his open window?

■ If you were the king, what would you say when Daniel got caught by the bad law you had signed?

■ What good things happened because of Daniel's faithfulness?

What can you say about Daniel? Lots of good things! But most of all, he was faithful to God. Let's see—what could Daniel have done when the king signed the law that people could pray only to him for the next 30 days? Well, he could have stopped praying in the window of his house. In a back room, no one would have seen him. Or he could have stared off into space as he prayed silently. That way no one could really tell he was praying. He even could have taken a break for 30 days. After all, it was only 30 days!

But no, Daniel kept on praying three times a day in the window of his house. That must have delighted his enemies, but it delighted God even more. Daniel knew the scriptures; he knew God's promises. He understood that his job was to be faithful to God and God would take care of the rest. Daniel knew God was bigger than any powerful plot, so he could trust God to protect him. And our ever faithful God did just that.

Bible Verse
For the LORD loves the just and will not forsake his faithful ones. They will be protected forever.
Psalm 37:28

Today in your shepherd groups you'll get to shut the lions' mouths yourselves!

Dismiss kids to their shepherd groups.

2 Shepherd's Spot

Gather your small group and help kids find Daniel 6 in their Bibles.

Daniel was an important official in a huge kingdom. The other leaders were jealous because the king loved Daniel and planned to put him in charge. So they hatched a sneaky plot to get the king to sign a law that would get Daniel in trouble for his faithfulness to God.

Have volunteers take turns reading Daniel 6:3–5, 7, 9-11, 13, 14, 16, 17, 19–23, 25, 26 aloud.

■ **Why didn't Daniel try to avoid trouble by praying in secret?**

■ **Have you ever felt like people were out to get you? What was that like?**

Daniel knew, and you need to know too, that when we are faithful to God, we can trust him to take care of everything else—even a den full of lions!

Pass out the "Well, Shut My Mouth!" handout and blank sheets of paper to serve as backing pieces. Have kids cut and assemble the lion whose mouth opens and closes according to the instructions on the handout. Ask a volunteer to read Psalm 37:28 aloud: *"For the LORD loves the just and will not forsake his faithful ones. They will be protected forever."*

■ **When is it tough for you to be faithful to God? What kinds of problems do you face?**

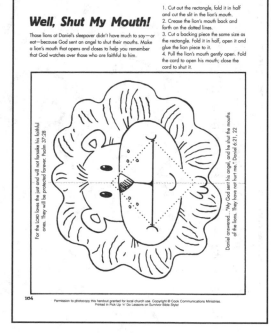

Let's imagine those problems going inside this lion's

mouth. Then close the card and WAP!—God takes care of the problems. When we're faithful to God, we're bound to run into difficult spots. But God watches over the faithful, just as he did Daniel.

Do you know some people who are faithful to God and need God's protection? Let's pray for them today. Dear Lord, we know that you are Lord of everything we see. You have been faithful and kind to us and we want to be faithful to you in everything we do. We thank you for the protection you promise to those who are faithful to you. Today we especially remember (name those kids mentioned). **We rely on your love and protection this week. In Jesus' name, amen.**

Permission to photocopy this lesson page granted for local church use. Copyright © Cook Communications Ministries.
Printed in Pick Up 'n' Do Lessons on Survivor Bible Style!

Well, Shut My Mouth!

Those lions at Daniel's sleepover didn't have much to say—or eat—because God sent an angel to shut their mouths. Make a lion's mouth that opens and closes to help you remember that God watches over those who are faithful to him.

1. Cut out the rectangle, fold it in half and cut the slit in the lion's mouth.
2. Crease the lion's mouth back and forth on the dotted lines.
3. Cut a backing piece the same size as the rectangle. Fold it in half, open it and glue the lion piece to it.
4. Pull the lion's mouth gently open. Fold the card to open his mouth; close the card to shut it.

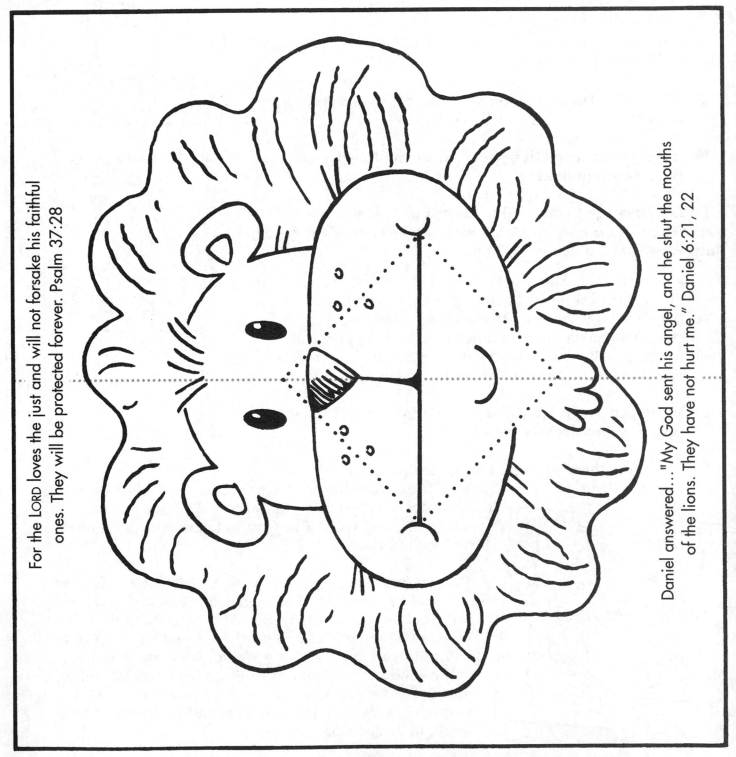

For the LORD loves the just and will not forsake his faithful ones. They will be protected forever. Psalm 37:28

Daniel answered... "My God sent his angel, and he shut the mouths of the lions. They have not hurt me." Daniel 6:21, 22

Permission to photocopy this handout granted for local church use. Copyright © Cook Communications Ministries.
Printed in Pick Up 'n' Do Lessons on Survivor Bible Style!

workshop Wonders

Gr-owwwww-l. Faithfulness to God is easier said than done when a lion comes to call! Daniel could have make things simple—stop praying to God or pray in secret. Both ways would have kept him safe. Instead Daniel remained loyal to God and he closed the lions' mouths. Today we're going to turn the tables and make yummy lions we can eat.

Get List:
- ☐ paper plates
- ☐ canned pear halves
- ☐ aerosol cream cheese spread
- ☐ chow mien noodles
- ☐ raisins
- ☐ Bugles® crackers
- ☐ spoons

1. Place a pear half, hollow side down, in the center of a paper plate. The wide part of the pear should be at the bottom.

2. Squirt cream cheese around the edge of the pear.

3. Press noodles into the cream cheese around the edges to make a "chow mane!"

4. Add raisins for eyes and a mouth.

5. Place a Bugle® cracker wide end down for the nose. If it's too long, bite off a piece of the wide end.

Discuss the story as kids make lion treats of their own.

■ **Do you think Daniel could hear the lions' restless snarls while he waited to be thrown in? How do you think he might have prayed?**

■ **Suppose you were Daniel's enemy and the stone had just sealed the lions' den closed. What would you have said?**

■ **A sleepover with hungry lions? No way! Yet Daniel did and stayed true to God. What do kids face today that make it tough to be faithful to God?** *(Popularity, cool clothes and things,"idol worship" of celebrities who choose wrong over right.)*

■ **How did Daniel's stand affect the powerful king of the day? How does it affect your friends when you choose to be faithful to God?**

Hand out spoons and let kids gobble their creations. As they leave, encourage kids to be faithful to God no matter what because they can trust God to protect them.

Lion Treat adapted from FUNtastic KidCrafts by Susan Parsons, published by Cook Communications Ministries. Used by permission.
Permission to photocopy this lesson page granted for local church use. Copyright © Cook Communications Ministries.
Printed in Pick Up 'n' Do Lessons on Survivor Bible Style!

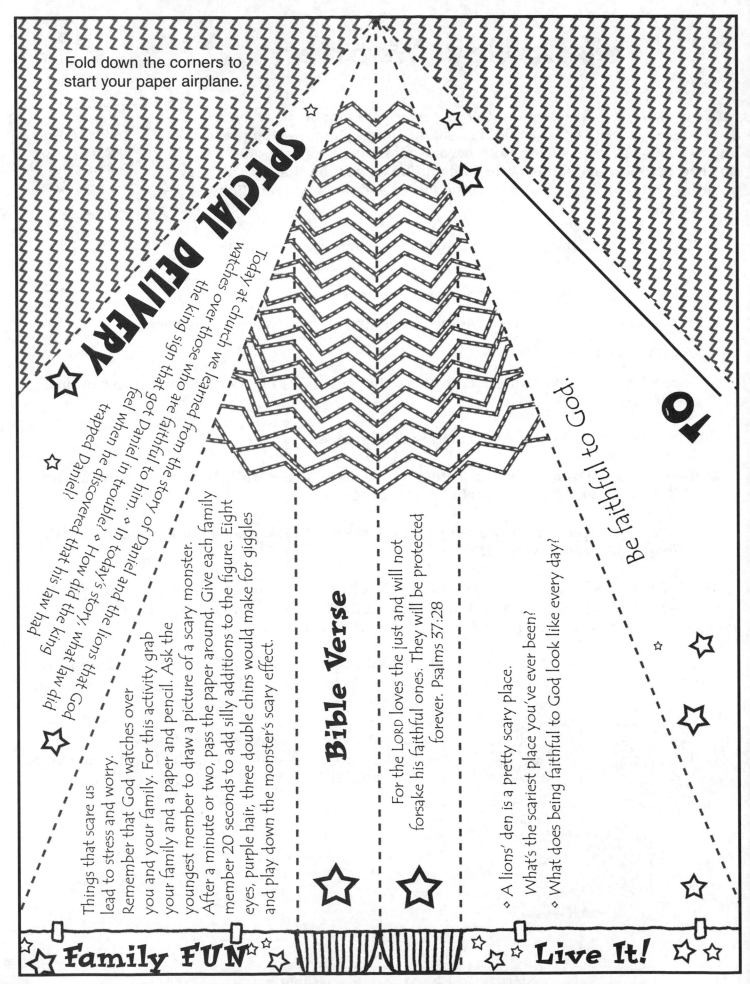

Fold down the corners to start your paper airplane.

SPECIAL DELIVERY

TO

Be faithful to God.

Family FUN

Things that scare us lead to stress and worry. Remember that God watches over you and your family. For this activity grab your family and a paper and pencil. Ask the youngest member to draw a picture of a scary monster. After a minute or two, pass the paper around. Give each family member 20 seconds to add silly additions to the figure. Eight eyes, purple hair, three double chins would make for giggles and play down the monster's scary effect.

Today at church we learned from the story of Daniel and the lions that God watches over those who are faithful to him. • In today's story, what law did the king sign that got Daniel in trouble? • How did the king feel when he discovered that his law had trapped Daniel?

Bible Verse

For the LORD loves the just and will not forsake his faithful ones. They will be protected forever. Psalms 37:28

Live It!

◇ A lions' den is a pretty scary place. What's the scariest place you've ever been?
◇ What does being faithful to God look like every day?

Permission to photocopy this handout granted for local church use. Copyright © Cook Communications Ministries. Printed in Pick Up 'n' Do Lessons on Survivor Bible Style!

Ambush!

Option — Get Set

LARGE GROUP ■ Greet kids and do a puppet skit. Schooner plans a fun excursion that leads into today's survivor Bible story.

❏ large bird puppet ❏ puppeteer

1 — Bible 4U! Instant Drama

LARGE GROUP ■ Paul's young nephew hears of an evil plot and alerts the Roman commander who arranges Paul's escape.

❏ 4 actors ❏ copies of pp. 110-111, On a Mission script ❏ 4 numbered balls
Optional: ❏ sunglasses ❏ coin ❏ Bibletime costumes ❏ night scene of a Bibletime street

2 — Shepherd's Spot

SMALL GROUP ■ Use the "Escape" handout to help kids re-create Paul's daring escape from Jerusalem.

❏ copies of p. 114, Escape! handout ❏ scissors ❏ glue ❏ fine-tipped markers
❏ copies of p. 116, Special Delivery

Option — Workshop Wonders

SMALL GROUP ■ A paper and scissors activity makes kids stretch their imaginations to explore today's "God makes a way for us" truth.

❏ masking tape ❏ paper ❏ scissors

Bible Basis
Paul escapes a plot.
Acts 21: 30, 33; 22:30;
23:1, 2, 10, 12, 13, 16,
19–24

Learn It!
God makes
a way for us.

Live It!
Be an agent
for God.

Bible Verse
It is God who arms me
with strength and makes
my way perfect.
2 Samuel 22:33

Quick Takes

Acts 21: 30, 33; 22:30; 23:1, 2, 10, 12, 13, 16, 19–24

21:30 The whole city was aroused, and the people came running from all directions. Seizing Paul, they dragged him from the temple, and immediately the gates were shut. 33 The commander came up and arrested him and ordered him to be bound with two chains. Then he asked who he was and what he had done.

22:30 The next day, since the commander wanted to find out exactly why Paul was being accused by the Jews, he released him and ordered the chief priests and all the Sanhedrin to assemble. Then he brought Paul and had him stand before them.

23:1 Paul looked straight at the Sanhedrin and said, "My brothers, I have fulfilled my duty to God in all good conscience to this day." 2 At this the high priest Ananias ordered those standing near Paul to strike him on the mouth.

10 The dispute became so violent that the commander was afraid Paul would be torn to pieces by them. He ordered the troops to go down and take him away from them by force and bring him into the barracks.

12 The next morning the Jews formed a conspiracy and bound themselves with an oath not to eat or drink until they had killed Paul.

13 More than forty men were involved in this plot.

16 But when the son of Paul's sister heard of this plot, he went into the barracks and told Paul.

19 The commander took the young man by the hand, drew him aside and asked, "What is it you want to tell me?"

20 He said: "The Jews have agreed to ask you to bring Paul before the Sanhedrin tomorrow on the pretext of wanting more accurate information about him.

21 Don't give in to them, because more than forty of them are waiting in ambush for him. They have taken an oath not to eat or drink until they have killed him. They are ready now, waiting for your consent to their request."

22 The commander dismissed the young man and cautioned him, "Don't tell anyone that you have reported this to me."

23 Then he called two of his centurions and ordered them, "Get ready a detachment of two hundred soldiers, seventy horsemen and two hundred spearmen to go to Caesarea at nine tonight.

24 Provide mounts for Paul so that he may be taken safely to Governor Felix."

Insights

Before Paul started on this trip to Jerusalem, several people tried to dissuade him. As a dynamic minister of the Gospel, trouble followed Paul wherever he went, and Jerusalem was certainly a hotbed of anti-Christian sentiment.

A hotly contested issue was whether Gentile Christians had to follow the Jewish rite of circumcision. Because Paul favored the Gentiles' freedom from such laws, his detractors riled up the crowd at the temple saying that Paul preached everywhere against the Jews and against the Law of Moses. Seeing the disturbance, the Romans intervened. Paul's arrest probably saved his life. While Paul was under Roman guard, a group of 40 assassins pledged not to eat or drink until they had killed Paul. Paul's young nephew heard of the plot and alerted the Roman commander who arranged Paul's escape with a guard of 470 soldiers! Thus began Paul's long journey to Rome.

It took courage for Paul's young nephew to speak to the Roman commander about the assassin's plot. And he did it so convincingly that the commander took extraordinary precaution to transfer Paul safely to Caesarea. Use this lesson to help kids understand that even though they're young, they can make a difference and help God's people.

Get Set

Outfit Schooner with a pair of sunglasses. Open with lively music, then greet the kids. **We like to get our way, don't we? My way is best. Your way is best. My way. Your way. That doesn't leave much room for God's perfect way. Schooner help me out here.** *Schooner pops up.*

Schooner: *(sings)* Over the river and through the woods to Grandmother's house we go…

Leader: Do you have a trip planned, Schooner?

Schooner: I surely do!

Leader: To your grandmother's?

Schooner: No. Grandma Wingnut hibernates this time of year.

Leader: Parrots hibernate?

Schooner: Retired ones do.

Leader: Ah. So why the shades?

Schooner: I'm on a mission.

Leader: What kind of a mission?

Schooner: A secret mission. Special Agent Schooner T. Parrot at your service.

Leader: Can you tell us anything about this mission?

Schooner: Then it wouldn't exactly be a secret, would it? *Squawk!*

Leader: You'd fit right in with today's Bible story.

Schooner: I just knew there had to be a parrot in the Bible somewhere!

Leader: This wasn't a parrot.

Schooner: *(sighs)* Fine. Who was it then? A secret agent with cool shades like mine?

Leader: Shades hadn't been invented yet. But this person did carry out a secret mission.

Schooner: Really? Was it a great rescuer? A mighty hero? A super spy?

Leader: A boy, actually. His mission was to get someone out of big trouble.

Schooner: Hmm. So where was the trouble?

Leader: In the middle of an angry crowd.

Schooner: Oh, no. Was the boy in the middle of the angry crowd?

Leader: Nope. His Uncle Paul was.

Schooner: Paul? Like Paul the preacher?

Leader: The very same. And a group of men plotted to kill him.

Schooner: OH, NO!

Leader: Just when things looked really bad, God used Paul's nephew to set the stage for a daring escape.

Schooner: So how did the boy help?

Leader: He overheard something about the plot.

Schooner: And then…

Leader: He told the leader of the Roman guards about it.

Schooner: Whoa—that took some courage. And some smarts!

Leader: Yep. He was just a boy but he was ready and willing to help. And he made a huge difference.

Schooner: Do you think a parrot could ever make a difference?

Leader: If any parrot could, it would be you, Schooner.

Schooner: Really?

Leader: Really! Listen carefully to today's Bible story and you might pick up some tips.

Schooner: I'm all ears!

Leader: Bible 4U! up next!

Permission to photocopy this script granted for local church use. Copyright © Cook Communications Ministries.
Printed in Pick Up 'n' Do Lessons on Survivor Bible Style!

1 Bible 4U!

After Paul had preached about Jesus far and wide, he decided to return to Jerusalem. His friends warned him not to. They knew the religious leaders in Jerusalem would be out to get him. And they were right. One day when Paul showed up in the temple, some members of the Sanhedrin recognized him. A huge fight broke out and they started beating Paul. The Romans saw what was going on and arrested Paul to save his life.

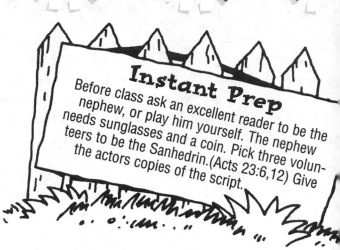

Instant Prep

Before class ask an excellent reader to be the nephew, or play him yourself. The nephew needs sunglasses and a coin. Pick three volunteers to be the Sanhedrin. (Acts 23:6,12) Give the actors copies of the script.

The Romans let Paul appear before the Sanhedrin and another fight broke out! They took him back to the barracks to question him and find out why he was always at the center of trouble. The religious leaders didn't want to let Paul slip through their fingers. So they made a plan to kill him.

for Overachievers

Have a four-person drama team prepare the script. Dress them in Bibletime costumes. Give the nephew sunglasses and a coin. Create a dark backdrop that suggests a Bibletime street at night.

Fortunately, Paul's young nephew overheard what was going on and took action to help. We learn from this story that people of all ages work for the will of God.

I see Paul's nephew now—let's see what he's discovered.

On a Mission
Based on Acts 21:27–23:31

Paul's nephew enters wearing dark sunglasses. He is taking quick glances around the room. He goes to center, looks left and right, sees audience, takes off glasses, and speaks.

Nephew: Oh, hello. I didn't see you there. You haven't seen anything suspicious have you? I am always on the lookout for my Uncle Paul. You've probably heard about him. He is the apostle who started out hating Jesus. But God changed his heart and now he preaches about Jesus everywhere he goes. Trouble is, not everyone is glad to hear about Jesus. Especially not here in Jerusalem. Things have been tense ever since he got here. In fact, he's in jail right now. The Romans arrested him for his own safety because the religious leaders were beating him and the soldiers thought he might be killed.

The next day Uncle Paul went before the Jewish leaders "My brothers, I have fulfilled my duty to God." The High Priest Ananias ordered his men to hit Paul in the mouth! Ouch! Uncle Paul was mad. He said. "God will strike you, you whitewashed walls!" That means they look good on the outside but are crummy on the inside. "You judge me by the law and then break the law by hitting me." Later he learned Ananias was a high priest, so he apologized.

Then a big argument broke out. Sparks flew and tempers flared! What a fight! It got so bad the Roman commander had to get Uncle Paul outta there fast. They took him back to the barracks for safety.

Three men of the Sanhedrin enter from the other side, talking quietly.

Nephew: Shh! Those are some of the men who are trying to make trouble for my uncle. They're up to no good, I can tell. I'm going to try to listen in on their plans.

He puts on sunglasses, goes stage right and crouches down as if hiding. The three go to center.

Man 1: What are we going to do about this Paul guy?

Man 2: We can't just let him keep preaching about Jesus. People will believe him and not us.

Man 3: We've got to rid of him any way we can.

Man 1: Let's get some other guys to help us. We can tell the Romans we want to question Paul some more. While he's on the way we can ambush him and kill him.

Man 2: It would take a lot of people to do that. He'll be under Roman protection.

Man 3: I bet I can get about forty guys together who would like to see Paul dead.

Man 1: That's the plan, then. I swear I won't eat or drink until Paul is dead.

Man 2: Me too.

Man 3: Me too.

Man 1: Okay, let's move out.

Nephew: *(to audience)* Did you hear that? They're going to have 40 guys in an ambush. Oh man, I've got to see if I can stop them.

But first I'll have to get past these guys.

Nephew tosses a coin downstage to one side of first man. He sees it and bends to pick it up.

Man 1: Hey, look what I found. Money!

The others go over to him to look, while Nephew sneaks the rest of the way. Men exit stage right, Nephew exits stage left. Nephew returns.

Nephew: I made it! I sneaked over to the Roman barracks, and because I'm just a kid, they let me in to see Uncle Paul. I told him what I'd heard about the ambush. He called over one of the soldiers and told him to take me to the commander.

The commander was big and tough looking, but I knew I had a mission and I couldn't let Uncle Paul down. I was scared, but I said a little prayer. The officer believed me! He was very concerned. We spoke in private so no one could overhear.

The commander acted quickly. First he dismissed me with this caution, "Don't tell anyone that you have reported this to me." Then he ordered a guard of two hundred soldiers, seventy horsemen, and two hundred spearmen to take Uncle Paul by horseback to another town where he would be safe. They made it safely past the ambush and out of town.

God let me play a role in Uncle Paul's escape. It never hurts to keep your eyes and ears open. Be a special agent for God and you never know how he will use you to help his people.

Permission to photocopy this script granted for local church use. Copyright © Cook Communications Ministries.
Printed in Pick Up 'n' Do Lessons on Survivor Bible Style!

Paul's nephew got to play in important role in Paul's escape. When he heard about the plot he acted quickly and wisely. And because God was with him, the Roman commander made a way to get Paul out of Jerusalem. Let's see if you can act quickly and wisely with these questions!

Toss the four numbered balls to different parts of the room. Bring kids with the balls to the front one-by-one and ask these questions. Allow kids to get help from the group if they need it. After each correct answer, let kids drop their balls into a bag.

■ Why did the religious leaders want to get rid of Paul?

■ How did Paul's nephew act as a special agent for God?

■ If you were one of Paul's enemies, what would you say when you found out about the 470 soldiers who guarded Paul on the way out of town?

■ What makes a person a good special agent for God?

The religious leaders in Jerusalem didn't succeed in killing Paul. Instead Paul continued to preach about Jesus in city after city. And he wrote letters to churches that we can find in our Bibles today. God used Paul's nephew as a special agent to help keep Paul alive. Maybe you think you are not strong enough or good enough or brave enough to be used by God but our Bible verse today tells us, "It is God who arms me with strength and makes my way   perfect."

God has something special for each of us to do. As his special agents we might help people who are in trouble, say a kind word to someone who's discouraged, or explain God's love and forgiveness to someone who's never heard. Keep your eyes and ears open. You never know when God might have a job for you. God makes a way for his people, and we can help, just as Paul's nephew did. Today in your shepherd groups you'll get to make a 3-D map that shows how God made a way for Paul to escape from Jerusalem.

Bible Verse
It is God who arms me with strength and makes my way perfect.
2 Samuel 22:33

Dismiss kids to their shepherd groups.

Gather your small group and help kids find Acts 21 in their Bibles.

Today's story is from the New Testament. It has been a while since Jesus died and wonderfully rose from the dead. The Good News about Jesus is spreading from country to country, and Paul is the main missionary. That's why so many people wanted to stop him.

Review the Bible story with your class and pass out the handouts.

■ **We don't really know how old Paul's nephew was. What would you guess?**

■ **Why does the verse say God makes our way perfect when troubles are always popping up?**

Plenty of perils awaited Paul in Jerusalem, but God made a way through them all! Color in the handout. Then cut apart, fold and glue the pieces of the "Escape!" handout to review the dangers Paul faced. Look at the cut-outs carefully before matching them to the scene at the bottom of the handout. A picture of the completed handout is shown below. You may wish to display it for kids to check their work. **Then let's follow the Bible verse as Paul makes his escape!**

I hope you'll look for ways to be God's agents this week. One thing we can do is pray for people who are facing troubles and ask God to make a way for them. Invite kids to mention people they'd like to pray for.

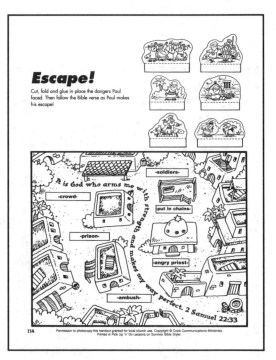

Then close with prayer. **Dear Lord, it's exciting to know that we can be agents for you. Help us keep our eyes and ears open for people who are going through hard times. Help us encourage them and remind them that you promise to make a way. We especially pray for** (mention the people kids named). **We trust that whatever we face this week, you'll make our way perfect. In Jesus' name, amen.**

Permission to photocopy this lesson page granted for local church use. Copyright © Cook Communications Ministries.
Printed in Pick Up 'n' Do Lessons on Survivor Bible Style!

Escape!

Cut, fold and glue in place the dangers Paul faced. Then follow the Bible verse as Paul makes his escape!

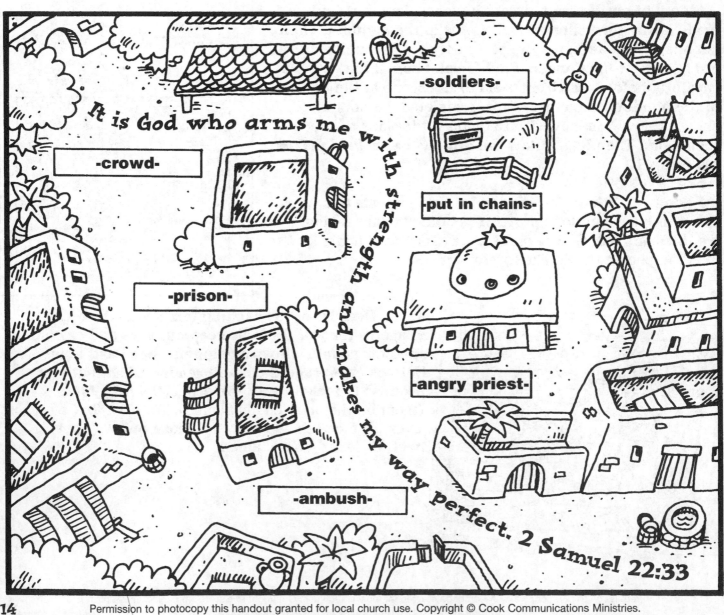

It is God who arms me with strength and makes my way perfect. 2 Samuel 22:33

-soldiers-

-crowd-

-put in chains-

-prison-

-angry priest-

-ambush-

Permission to photocopy this handout granted for local church use. Copyright © Cook Communications Ministries.
Printed in Pick Up 'n' Do Lessons on Survivor Bible Style!

Paul was in a pretty tight fix. Men waited in hiding to kill him. Things were looking pretty bad. But God had his own secret agent and he would make a way for Paul.

Get List:
- ❑ masking tape
- ❑ paper
- ❑ scissors

■ **Can you remember a time when an "agent for God" helped you find a way through a tough spot? What did he or she do for you?**

As you introduce today's Workshop Wonder activity to your class, place two parallel pieces of masking tape on the floor about four feet apart. **Sometimes it looks like there just isn't any way things will work out. And in human hands there isn't. In such times we need God's help. Let's try a little mission of our own now. I need some agents who are ready for a challenging task.**

Have your kids buddy up. Give each pair a piece of plain paper and a pair of scissors. **I'd like you to stretch your paper to "make a way" from one of these tape lines to the other. Helpful hint: You may cut the paper. But do not remove any pieces. In other words, the paper must stay connected and in one piece.**

A few of your kids may figure out this paper trick. If they do, say, **I see some pretty smart special agents!"**

After a few minutes, show all the children the two ways they can stretch their papers.

Method 1: Make alternating cuts from the long sides of the paper stopping just short of the other side.
Method 2: Cut the paper in a spiral pattern.

Have fresh paper on hand for extra attempts. Challenge the class to see whose paper stretches the farthest. **It is pretty amazing how far our papers stretched when we knew just the right cuts to make.**

God knows the way to make things work. Sometimes he chooses special agents to do the job. In our story Paul's nephew was the one God chose for the job.

■ **I appoint you a not-so-secret agent for God! What special tools did God give you that you might use to help out others in a tight spot?**

Nothing is impossible for God. Let's remember today's Bible verse to keep God's wisdom in mind—always.

"It is God who arms me with strength and makes my way perfect." 2 Samuel 22:33

Fold down the corners to start your paper airplane.

SPECIAL DELIVERY

TO

God makes a way for us.
Be an agent for God.

Today at church we learned that God makes a way for us, Who set up an ambush? Why did they want to kill Paul? Name different people or groups who played a role in Paul's escape from Jerusalem.

Family FUN

Secret plots and secret plans did not spell disaster for the Apostle Paul. God made a way to save him. Use a hand mirror or mirrored dresser in your home for this little coded message trick. Lay the paper on the dresser so you can see it in the mirror. Now write backward! That is, print a message that looks right when you look in the mirror. "God makes a way" would make a great message. Now deliver your message to a family member to decode. How? Hold the paper up to a mirror!

Bible Verse

It is God who arms me with strength and makes my way perfect.
2 Samuel 22:33

Live It!

◊ The religious leaders were angry because Paul was teaching about Jesus. Do people today get in trouble for telling about Jesus? How can we help them?

◊ How do you feel when someone helps you out of a tight spot (like Paul's nephew did for Paul in today's story)?

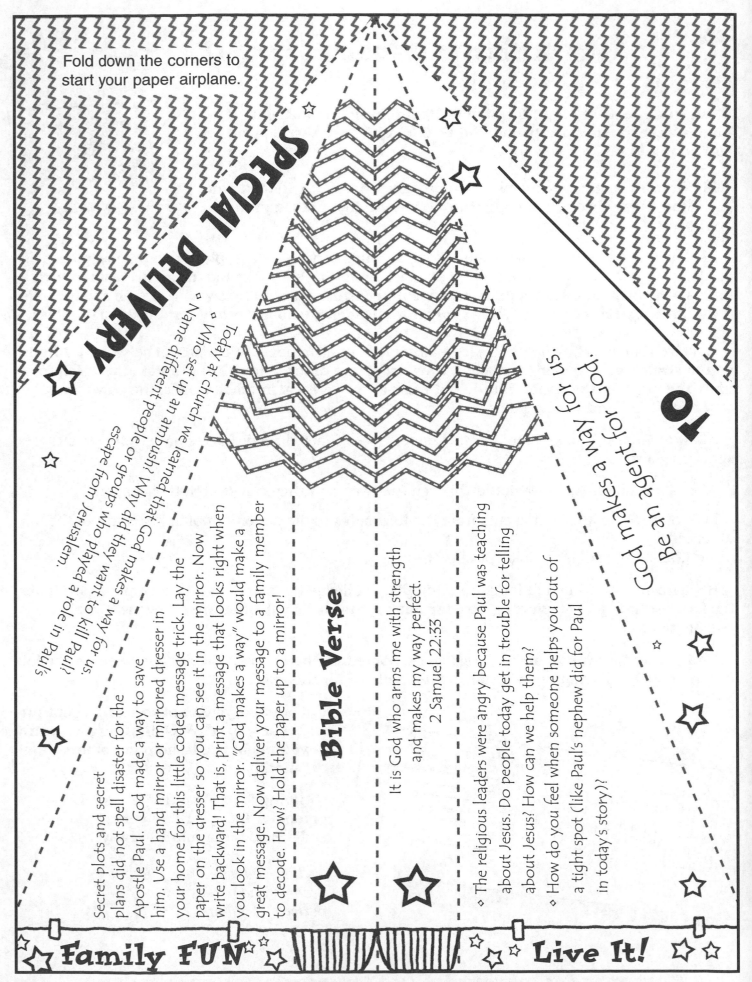

Permission to photocopy this handout granted for local church use. Copyright © Cook Communications Ministries.
Printed in Pick Up 'n' Do Lessons on Survivor Bible Style!

Storm Warning

Option

Get Set
LARGE GROUP ■ Greet kids and do a puppet skit. Schooner learns the value of being patient.

❑ *large bird puppet* ❑ *puppeteer*

1

Bible 4U! Instant Drama
LARGE GROUP ■ Today's story finds Paul on a long sea voyage to Rome.

❑ *3 actors* ❑ *copies of pp. 120-121, Here's Hope! script* ❑ *4 numbered balls*
Optional: ❑ *Bibletime costumes* ❑ *boxes* ❑ *coiled rope* ❑ *fans* ❑ *spray water*

2

Shepherd's Spot
SMALL GROUP ■ Use the "Hope Floats!" handout to help kids learn that there's always hope when we keep our trust in God.

❑ *Bibles* ❑ *pencils* ❑ *scissors* ❑ *copies of p. 124, Hope Floats!* ❑ *copies of p. 126, Special Delivery*

Option

Workshop Wonders
SMALL GROUP ■ Make extra-special gift bags for food pantry guests.

❑ *paper lunch bags* ❑ *rubber stamps/ink pads* ❑ *stickers* ❑ *gel pens*
❑ *small packaged food and personal care items*

Bible Basis
Paul survives a shipwreck.
Acts 27:1, 14, 18–26, 33–36, 42–44

Learn It!
God's people give hope and comfort.

Live It!
Give hope and comfort.

Bible Verse
Be strong and take heart, all you who hope in the LORD.
Psalm 31:24

Quick Takes

27:1 When it was decided that we would sail for Italy, Paul and some other prisoners were handed over to a centurion named Julius, who belonged to the Imperial Regiment.

14 Before very long, a wind of hurricane force, called the "north-easter", swept down from the island.

18 We took such a violent battering from the storm that the next day they began to throw the cargo overboard.

19 On the third day, they threw the ship's tackle overboard with their own hands.

20 When neither sun nor stars appeared for many days and the storm continued raging, we finally gave up all hope of being saved.

21 After the men had gone a long time without food, Paul stood up before them and said: "Men, you should have taken my advice not to sail from Crete; then you would have spared yourselves this damage and loss.

22 But now I urge you to keep up your courage, because not one of you will be lost; only the ship will be destroyed.

23 Last night an angel of the God whose I am and whom I serve stood beside me

24 and said, 'Do not be afraid, Paul. You must stand trial before Caesar; and God has graciously given you the lives of all who sail with you.'

25 So keep up your courage, men, for I have faith in God that it will happen just as he told me.

26 Nevertheless, we must run aground on some island."

33 Just before dawn Paul urged them all to eat. "For the last fourteen days," he said, "you have been in constant suspense and have gone without food—you haven't eaten anything.

34 Now I urge you to take some food. You need it to survive. Not one of you will lose a single hair from his head."

35 After he said this, he took some bread and gave thanks to God in front of them all. Then he broke it and began to eat.

36 They were all encouraged and ate some food themselves.

42 The soldiers planned to kill the prisoners to prevent any of them from swimming away and escaping.

43 But the centurion wanted to spare Paul's life and kept them from carrying out their plan. He ordered those who could swim to jump overboard first and get to land.

44 The rest were to get there on planks or on pieces of the ship. In this way everyone reached land in safety.

Insights

Luke's detailed account puts us smack in the middle of a sea voyage gone terribly wrong. Paul's journey to Rome as a prisoner took him along the coast of modern-day Turkey and finally to the island of Crete. It was late fall, and approaching violent winter storms made travel on the Mediterranean treacherous. Some, including Paul, wanted to winter at Crete and sail on in spring when the weather was dependable. But the decision was made to sail west, and soon the huge grain ship found itself in the teeth of a savage two-week storm.

The sailors who wanted to desert the ship and take to the boats were stopped. The ship's crew took every drastic measure, but after days of terror it became evident that the ship would wreck against the island of Malta. When everyone was filled with despair in the face of what they thought was imminent death, Paul stood and brought words of comfort and encouragement. He had everyone eat and told them that though the ship would wreck, they would all survive. His words and actions gave hope, and by God's grace everyone aboard the ship survived the wreck.

One comforting, encouraging voice can make a world of difference to people who are filled with despair. Use this lesson to teach kids that because their hope is in the Lord, they can be strong and take heart in any situation, and pass their hope and strength to others.

Get Set

Open with lively music, then greet the kids. **People with big hearts are great! What would we do without them? These special people give us hope and comfort and help us keep the faith through our "survivor" times.** Schooner, come up and say hello. *Schooner pops up.*

Schooner: How about a back rub, boss?

Leader: *(rubs Schooner's back)* How does that feel?

Schooner: *(sighs)* Like butter. I'm melting!

Leader: You certainly feel tense today, Schooner.

Schooner: I'm nervous, boss. I start swimming lessons this afternoon.

Leader: I thought parrots didn't swim.

Schooner: I have a friend who wants to learn.

Leader: And?

Schooner: And I said I would encourage her.

Leader: That's wonderful, Schooner.

Schooner: So I signed up too.

Leader: It sounds like you're ready to go!

Schooner: Just me and my brand-new goose feather bathing suit.

Leader: I'm not even going to ask! Learning to swim is an important skill to have.

Schooner: But there's a problem.

Leader: Yes?

Schooner: I'm the only parrot in class.

Leader: Oh.

Schooner: So the life preserver will be much too big.

Leader: Hmm.

Schooner: And no one will pay attention to me.

Leader: *(shakes head)*

Schooner: I'll get splashed a lot.

Leader: I see.

Schooner: And, worst of all, parrots float.

Leader: That's good, isn't it?

Schooner: Not if you want to learn to swim under water.

Leader: Schooner, I don't think you need to worry. The kids will love you, we do! *(have the group clap to encourage Schooner)*

Schooner: *(nods head shyly)*

Leader: The teacher will love you too. *(hugs Schooner)*

Schooner: *(giggles)*

Leader: And you and your friend are sure to have fun learning together.

Schooner: Okay. I'll do my best!

Leader: There you go.

Schooner: Thanks for the words of comfort, boss.

Leader: God asks us to do that, Schooner. Give each other hope and comfort.

Schooner: It really helps.

Leader: Apostle Paul comforted his shipmates in today's storm-at-sea Bible story.

Schooner: A storm at sea? Whoosh. Whoosh. Who-o-o-o.

Leader: An awful storm.

Schooner: Paul sounds like a great guy, boss.

Leader: I agree.

Schooner: He places his trust in God no matter what trouble he's in.

Leader: We've seen the Apostle Paul in quite a few spots, haven't we?

Schooner: Hot spots and sore spots! *Squawk!*

Leader: Psalm 31:24 tell us to, "Be strong and take heart, all you who hope in the Lord."

Schooner: I will keep today's Bible verse in mind for this afternoon's swim.

Leader: God's Word—the best life preserver around. And one size fits all!

Schooner: I get it! Good one, boss.

Schooner and Leader: Bible 4U! up next.

Permission to photocopy this script granted for local church use. Copyright © Cook Communications Ministries.
Printed in Pick Up 'n' Do Lessons on Survivor Bible Style!

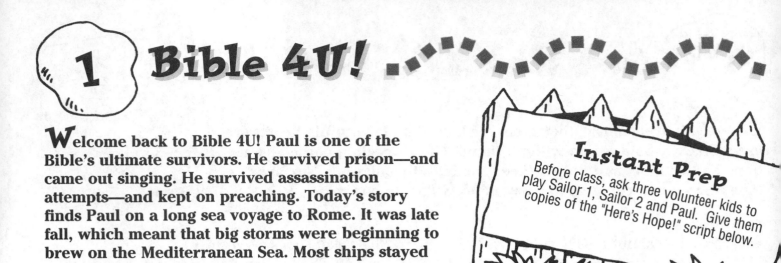

1 Bible 4U!

Welcome back to Bible 4U! Paul is one of the Bible's ultimate survivors. He survived prison—and came out singing. He survived assassination attempts—and kept on preaching. Today's story finds Paul on a long sea voyage to Rome. It was late fall, which meant that big storms were beginning to brew on the Mediterranean Sea. Most ships stayed safely in port through the winter. But the people on Paul's ship decided to sail on.

Instant Prep
Before class, ask three volunteer kids to play Sailor 1, Sailor 2 and Paul. Give them copies of the "Here's Hope!" script below.

You can probably guess what happened, but you won't have to because we're going to board the ship ourselves. It's just getting ready to leave its port on the island of Crete.

for Overachievers
Have a three-person drama team prepare the story. Dress them in Bibletime costumes. Set out boxes and coiled rope to create a ship's atmosphere. Have helpers turn on fans and spray water to create storm effects.

Did you bring your luggage and sunscreen? A sturdy pair of comfortable walking shoes? An umbrella for the big storm and a pair of rain boots? Sorry. No time to run back and get them.

Hurry come with me. If we run, we can just make it…

Here's Hope!
Based on Acts 27:1, 14, 18–26, 33–36, 42–44

Sailor 1: Hey, I haven't seen you before. Welcome aboard.
Sailor 2: Thanks. This is my first voyage.
Sailor 1: She's a fine ship, isn't she? Two hundred seventy-six passengers and tons of grain in the hold.
Sailor 2: *(sways a bit)* Ooh—we must have pulled out of port. Everything is rocking and swaying. My stomach feels—oh, my! *(runs off stage)*
Sailor 1: *(to audience, laughing)* Always happens to first-timers. He'll get his sea legs in a day or two.

Sailor 2 enters.

Sailor 1: Feeling better?
Sailor 2: A little—sort of. So, tell me about these passengers. Who's that guy with the Roman Centurion? At first I thought he was a prisoner, but everyone treats him with respect.
Sailor 1: That would be Paul. You're right on both counts. He is a prisoner and he does get treated with a lot of respect.
Sailor 2: Is he rich or something?
Sailor 1: No. He's an apostle of the Jewish prophet, Jesus. Have you heard of him?

Sailor 2: Was he the one they killed thirty or forty years ago?

Sailor 1: Yes, but according to Paul, he rose from the dead. He says Jesus is the Son of God and that people who believe in him will be saved from their sins.

Sailor 2: Do you believe that stuff?

Sailor 1: I've been thinking a lot about it. I hope to hear more of what Paul has to say during this voyage.

Both sailors fall to one side.

Sailor 2: What was THAT?

Sailor 1: A northeaster. We're in for a nasty storm. I was worried about this. Some said it was too late in the year to sail for Rome.

They stand, then fall to the other side. Helpers turn on fans and begin spraying water.

Sailor 2: I don't like this at all. I should have listened to my mother. She wanted me to stay home and work on the farm.

Sailor 1: We'll just have to ride this out.

They hunch on the floor and sway back and forth with the waves six times. Then they stand, shaking and hanging on to each other.

Sailor 2: Do you think we're going to make it?

Sailor 1: Honestly, no. I don't. We've been riding the storm for fourteen days now. We've done everything we can to save the ship.

Sailor 2: We tossed the cargo...

Sailor 1: We wrapped ropes around the hull...

Sailor 2: The ship can't stand much more of this, can it?

Sailor 1: It's going to break apart any minute now. Or else we'll crash right into that island.

Sailor 2: We're going to die!

Sailor 1: There's no hope!

The sailors sob. Paul enters.

Paul: Take heart, my friends. An angel appeared to me and told me that the ship will crash, but we'll all survive. Now eat something. You'll need your strength. I have faith that God will do just what he promised—not one of us will be lost!

Sailor 1: I believe him—and I believe in his God!

Sailor 2: We might make it after all.

Sailor 1: Look! There's a sandy beach! The captain will try to run her aground over there.

Both sailors lurch.

Sailor 2: We hit a sandbar, didn't we?

Sailor 1: Yes, but we're not far from shore. Are you a good swimmer?

Sailor 2: Sort of.

Sailor 1: Jump!

Both leap and flap their arms.

Both: Ahhhhhhhhhhh!

They "swim" offstage. Paul enters.

Paul: The ship broke apart just off the island of Malta. But, just as God said, all 276 people on board made it to shore.

Sailors enter and speak to Paul.

Sailor 1: Paul, um...sir. I want to thank you for giving us hope back there.

Sailor 2: I was sure we were goners. But you said we would all be saved. And then the beach appeared. And even the people who couldn't swim were able to float in on pieces of the boat.

Paul: God is merciful, my friends.

Sailor 1: Speaking of God, after what happened, I believe in him.

Sailor 2: Me too.

Sailor 1: And we'd both like to hear more about Jesus.

Paul: Come over here by the fire and I'll tell you all about the Son of God.

They exit.

Permission to photocopy this script granted for local church use. Copyright © Cook Communications Ministries.
Printed in *Pick Up 'n' Do Lessons on Survivor Bible Style!*

How amazing is it that a huge ship would break apart at sea and all 276 people aboard would swim or float safely to shore in the middle of a vicious storm? God gave hope through Paul, and no one was disappointed. Let's see what you understand about that hope.

Toss the four numbered balls to different parts of the room. Bring the kids with the balls to the front one-by-one and ask these questions. Allow kids to get help from the group if they need it. After each correct answer, let kids drop their balls into a bag.

■ You're a sailor on the ship. The storm is so bad you've had to throw most of your cargo overboard just to stay afloat. What are you thinking?

■ Paul told everyone to eat—that the ship would crash and break apart, but everyone would survive. Do you think they believed him? Why or why not?

■ Tell about a time you were sad or afraid and a friend comforted you and gave you hope.

■ Do you think Christians can always give hope? Explain.

How many of you have been on a ship in a bad storm? Pretty scary, isn't it? You lurch back and forth and waves wash clear over the boat. Even if you're in a big storm on land that goes on for days and days, it's easy to start thinking you'll never see the sun again. Wind whips the trees, rain drives against the windows and everything is gloomy, dark and drippy. Then someone knocks at your door, comes in with big beaming smile and says, "Isn't this rain just wonderful? The farmers have needed water so badly and the rivers are getting back to normal. Does anybody want to grab some boots and a jacket and go stomp in the mud puddles with me?" Suddenly the day looks completely different!

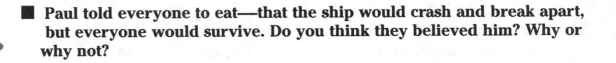

Bible Verse
Be strong and take heart, all you who hope in the LORD.
Psalm 31:24

One person with a hopeful attitude can make a HUGE difference. Unfortunately, one really gloomy person can have the same effect. But we are people of God, so we're people of hope. When we keep our eyes focused on what God can do, we can offer hope and comfort in any situation. Today in your shepherd groups you'll discover why Christians have unsinkable hope!

Dismiss kids to their shepherd groups.

Gather your small group and help kids find Acts 27 in their Bibles.

Paul is at it again, in the middle of another crisis! But he's not a bit scared. How can that be? Let's find out.

Write these scripture references on slips of paper and have volunteers take turns reading the passages aloud: Acts 27:1, 14, 18–26, 33–36, 42–44.

■ **The people on the ship felt that all was lost. Have you ever felt that way?**

■ **Do you know someone who seems to make everyone around him or her feel hopeful? What is that person like?**

As Christians, the hope we have to give is real. It's not just putting on a brave face. It comes from our faith in God.

Pass out the "Hope Floats!" handout. Have a volunteer read the verse on the waves aloud: *"Be strong and take heart, all you who hope in the LORD"* (Psalm 31:24).

Not even a fourteen-day storm at sea could sink Paul's hope! Have kids cut out and assemble the floating boat according to the instructions on the handout. Open and close the finished piece. **Look, the sea wants to swallow it up, but it pops right back up again. The hope that God gives us stays afloat in every storm, disaster and problem that life sends because we know that God is in control and that he loves us. Hope is a gift from God to you—a gift he wants you to pass on to others.**

Let's pray for people who need hope this week. Let kids share their prayer concerns. Then close with prayer. **Dear God of all hope, we know you are there, guiding and taking care of us even when life's storms are at their very worst. Help us keep our hope anchored in** you. **Then let us comfort others with that hope. We pray for** (mention kids' concerns). **Thank you for keeping us afloat in the safety of your love. In Jesus' name, amen.**

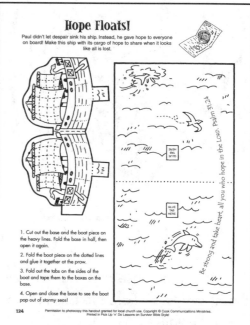

Hope Floats!

Paul didn't let despair sink his ship. Instead, he gave hope to everyone on board! Make this ship with its cargo of hope to share when it looks like all is lost.

1. Cut out the base and the boat piece on the heavy lines. Fold the base in half, then open it again.

2. Fold the boat piece on the dotted lines and glue it together at the prow.

3. Fold out the tabs on the sides of the boat and tape them to the boxes on the base.

4. Open and close the base to see the boat pop out of stormy seas!

124   Permission to photocopy this handout granted for local church use. Copyright © Cook Communications Ministries.
Printed in Pick Up 'n' Do Lessons on Survivor Bible Style!

Be strong and take heart, all you who hope in the LORD. Psalm 31:24

Permission to photocopy this lesson page granted for local church use. Copyright © Cook Communications Ministries.
Printed in Pick Up 'n' Do Lessons on Survivor Bible Style!

Hope Floats!

Paul didn't let despair sink his ship. Instead, he gave hope to everyone on board! Make this ship with its cargo of hope to share when it looks like all is lost.

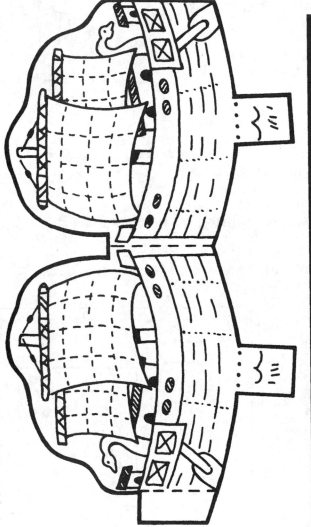

GLUE TAB HERE

GLUE TAB HERE

Be strong and take heart, all you who hope in the LORD. Psalm 31:24

1. Cut out the base and the boat piece on the heavy lines. Fold the base in half, then open it again.

2. Fold the boat piece on the dotted lines and glue it together at the prow.

3. Fold out the tabs on the sides of the boat and tape them to the boxes on the base.

4. Open and close the base to see the boat pop out of stormy seas!

Permission to photocopy this handout granted for local church use. Copyright © Cook Communications Ministries.
Printed in Pick Up 'n' Do Lessons on Survivor Bible Style!

Workshop Wonders

Paul climbed into a ship headed for Rome. It wasn't like the little fishing vessels Jesus and his disciples used. This was a huge ship used to carry grain across the Mediterranean Sea to Rome. But the voyage started too late in the season and the ship sailed right into the teeth of a raging storm.

Get List:
- ❏ paper lunch bags
- ❏ rubber stamps/ink pads
- ❏ stickers, gel pens
- ❏ small packaged food and personal care items

■ Do you have a special Bible passage that gives you comfort when you're frightened or unsure of what to do next? Share it with the class.

Hurricane force winds whipped the air and wild waves crashed over the sides of the boat. The boat rocked back and forth threatening to turn over and spill them all out into the black, rushing water.

■ What's the worst storm you can remember? How did it make you feel?

■ From the people you know, who would you pick to be at your side when a big storm hits? How would he or she comfort you?

You can imagine what the men on that ship were feeling. They were in a really tough spot and scared out of their wits. But God delivered to Paul a message of hope and comfort to share—"You'll make it." And they did. We can give comfort to others wherever we are. A storm in the middle of the ocean. A classroom. On the swings in the backyard. Hope and comfort is ours to give because God comforts us.

Make comfort bags to share with those who visit your local food bank. **People who visit the food bank are often in the middle of tough times. They come discouraged. We want to fill our bags with special things that will pick them up and make them feel comforted and extra cared for.**

Have kids print Psalm 31:24 on the bags, then decorate them and fill them with the things you've gathered. You may want to have kids add a brief note such as "Prepared for you by Emily." (If you feel that adding a name to the note places your kids at risk with strangers do not add it. If you do, make sure no one adds a last name.)

"Be strong and take heart, all you who hope in the LORD."
Psalm 31:24

Be on the lookout for times you can offer comfort and hope this week! If you have a food pantry located within your church building, let the kids help deliver the bags they've prepared.

Permission to photocopy this lesson page granted for local church use. Copyright © Cook Communications Ministries.
Printed in Pick Up 'n' Do Lessons on Survivor Bible Style!

Fold down the corners to start your paper airplane.

SPECIAL DELIVERY

TO

Give hope and comfort.

"How did Paul help make everyone "survivors"?

"Describe what happened on Paul's sea voyage.

Today at church we learned that God's people give hope and comfort.

Family FUN

Comfort food makes you feel warm and cozy inside. Make a batch of cheese puffs and comfort your family on a down-weather day. Combine 1 lb. of shredded cheddar cheese with 3 cups of biscuit baking mix and 3/4 cup of water. Mix well. Roll the mixture into balls and place on a baking sheet. With your parents help, bake at 400° for 12 minutes. Serve warm—with glasses of stormy water (soda or other fizzy beverage!) and a Bible open to Acts 27.

Bible Verse

Be strong and take heart, all you who hope in the LORD.
Psalms 31:24

Live It!

◇ Which would you prefer? To give hope and comfort or to receive hope and comfort? Why?

◇ If you were to write a prescription for hope and encouragement, what would it include? A hug? Kind words? A cup of hot chocolate? A note? A special Bible verse?

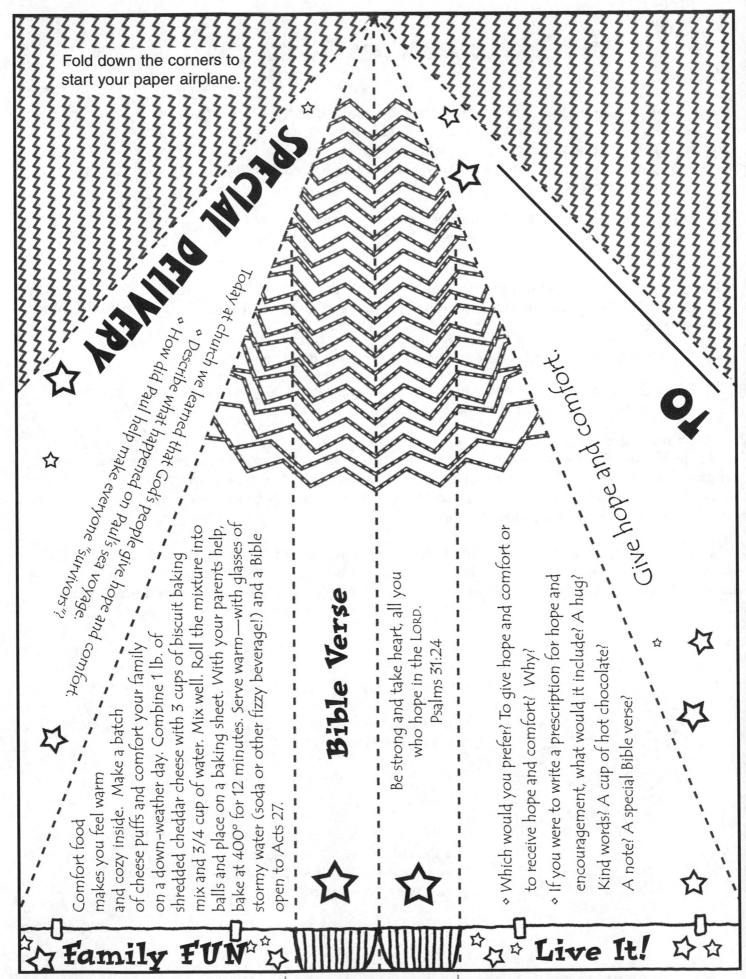

Permission to photocopy this handout granted for local church use. Copyright © Cook Communications Ministries.
Printed in Pick Up 'n' Do Lessons on Survivor Bible Style!